MYSTICS

MURRAY BODO

mystics

TEN WHO
SHOW US
THE WAYS
OF GOD

ST. ANTHONY MESSENGER PRESS
Cincinnati, Ohio

Excerpts from *St. Francis of Assisi: Writings and Early Documents: English Omnibus for the Sources of the Life of St. Francis*, Marion A. Habig, ed., ©1973, used by permission of Franciscan Press, Quincy, Illinois. All rights reserved. Excerpts from *Revelations of Divine Love*, translated by Clifton Wolters, copyright ©1966, used by permission of the translator. Excerpts from *Jacopone da Todi: The Lauds*, translated by Serge and Elizabeth Hughes, copyright ©1982, used by permission of Paulist Press, www.paulistpress.com. Excerpts from *Catherine of Siena: The Dialogue*, translated by Suzanne Noffke, O.P., copyright ©1980, used by permission of Paulist Press, www.paulistpress.com. Excerpts from *The Autobiography of St. Thérèse of Lisieux: The Story of a Soul*, by St. Thérèse of Lisieux, translated by John Beevers, copyright ©1957, by Doubleday, a division of Random House, Inc. Excerpts from *Story of a Soul*, translated by John Clarke, O.C.D., copyright ©1975, 1976, 1996 by Washington Province of Discalced Carmelites, used by permission of ICS Publications, www.icspublications.org. Excerpts from *Gerard Manley Hopkins: Poems and Prose*, W.H. Gardner, ed., ©1984, used by permission of Oxford University Press, www.oup.com. Excerpts from *Waiting for God*, by Simone Weil, translated by Emma Craufurd, copyright ©1951, renewed 1979 by G.P. Putnam's Sons used by permission of G.P. Putnam's Sons, a division of Penguin Group (USA) Inc. Excerpts from the writings of Robert Lax are used by permission of Marcia Kelly for the Estate of Robert Lax.
Scripture passages have been taken from *New Revised Standard Version Bible*, copyright ©1989 by the Division of Christian Education of the National Council of the Churches of Christ in the U.S.A., and used by permission. All rights reserved.

Cover and book design by Mark Sullivan
Cover image ©www.istockphoto.com/Eva Serrabassa

LIBRARY OF CONGRESS CATALOGING-IN-PUBLICATION DATA
Bodo, Murray.
Mystics : 10 who show us the ways of God / Murray Bodo.
p. cm.
Includes bibliographical references and index.
ISBN 978-0-86716-746-7 (pbk. : alk. paper) 1. Mystics—Biography. I. Title.
BV5095.A1B63 2007
248.2'20922—dc22
[B]
2007025738

ISBN 978-0-86716-746-7

Published by St. Anthony Messenger Press
28 W. Liberty St.
Cincinnati, OH 45202
www.AmericanCatholic.org

Printed in the United States of America.

Printed on acid-free paper.

07 08 09 10 11   5 4 3 2 1

For Herbert Lomas

Since, tho' he is under the world's splendour and wonder,
His mystery must be instressed, stressed;
For I greet him the days I meet him, and bless when I understand.

—Gerard Manley Hopkins,
"The Wreck of the Deutschland"

contents

How the Mystics Show Us the Ways of God

When I first began to read the mystics, I was troubled and not a little frightened at how much they suffered. It was almost as if they wanted to suffer, or God wanted them to suffer. At length, however, I came to realize that though we all suffer, the saint and mystic somehow move through suffering very little self-preoccupied. In fact, often he or she is occupied with work that even a healthy person would find daunting. Saint Francis of Assisi, for example, was intensely occupied in evangelizing, and Saint Teresa of Avila was busy founding new monasteries to the very end of her life, despite serious illness.

The saints' preoccupation is with others: the Other, God, most of all, but also their neighbor, society at large. They live with their eyes fixed on God and their neighbor; they become living examples of what it means to love God with one's whole heart and mind and soul and to love one's neighbor as oneself. So it is not the suffering that is the point of the lives of saints and mystics; it is that suffering and illness do not keep them from loving God and neighbor. Their gaze is outward

1

from the place inside where they dwell almost constantly in God's presence.

This inner absorption in God does not keep the saint inside, rapt in God and unaware of others; it may for awhile, during the time of ecstasy or inner vision, but inevitably absorption in God leads to a greater perception of outward things that makes of the saint and mystic one who serves and loves others to a heroic degree. Charity is what makes saints and mystics, not the inner visions, marvels or miracles. "[F]aith, hope, and love abide," Saint Paul says, "and the greatest of these is love" (1 Corinthians 13:13). Theirs is a love that manifests itself outwardly in this way: "[T]he fruit of the Spirit is love, joy, peace, patience, kindness, generosity, faithfulness, gentleness, and self-control" (Galatians 5:22).

The difficult balancing act of the mystic, as with all who want to live intimately with God, is how to live in the world but not be of the world, to love one's body but not let the body dominate the spirit, to love life but not let love of life keep one from longing for eternity. And thus begins asceticism, those practices that endeavor to free the person from being dominated by this world's needs and pleasures to the exclusion of what is eternal and spiritual. But here is where extremes can proliferate. Saints, human beings that they are, go to extremes at times, thinking that punishing the body or world-centered impulses will necessarily result in spiritual absorption. It may or may not, depending on the motivation, which could be anything from self-hatred and fear of the body, to slavish imitation of other saints who are misunderstood. Saints do make mistakes.

Toward the end of his life, Saint Francis of Assisi, the gentlest of saints, asked forgiveness of his own Brother Body. As a young man swept up in the enthusiasm of his conversion, he had dubbed it Brother Ass and had required great sacrifices from it. His initial penances were as much to punish himself for his earlier worldly excesses as they were attempts to grow closer to Christ. As he grew closer to Christ, he came to see that it is not self-imposed suffering that matters, but as with Christ himself, it is surrender to God's will out of love of God, whatever that will asks of us. That surrender brings its own pain and suffering because of our human condition and because of human sin. Even Jesus suffered at the hands of those who were not united to God's will.

In his "Canticle of the Creatures," Saint Francis says, "Blessed are those whom death will find in your most holy will, for *the second death* shall do them no harm."[1] He does not say, "Blessed are those who have done penances," but "Blessed are those who are found in his most holy will."

The moment of ecstasy for all mystics is the moment of God's entrance into their lives, an experience so intense that they are aware of nothing except the infinity of God's love, and they want nothing but to submit themselves to the will of that love—the source of all bliss, of all fulfillment and enlightenment and peace. In order to keep attuned to that will, mystics are much concerned not to let preoccupation with self or with the material blind them. They are perpetually aware that their experience of God was completely gratuitous, that it was not merited but was pure grace. Though some are graced to have this experience more than once, it is not something that can be repeated at will; it must be lovingly recalled at all times, like a cherished and life-changing memory.

At times, in going too far, they discover that penance itself can be a new god, blinding them to the will of the God they love and want to

3

serve. Saints grow, as do all human beings, and learn that penance is not the point; the will of God is—a will that is motivated by the eternal, overflowing love of God, who wants only the best for the beloved creature that is the fruit of the Love that results from the eternal interaction of the Holy Trinity.

We read the mystics for the same reason we read the Bible, because we find there an articulation of intimacy with God. Abraham and Moses have experiences of God; the writers of Genesis and Exodus relate the experiences. The prophets experience God; their prophecies find words to express that experience. We read the prophets to learn what God told them. But we also read, hoping, through them, to have a vicarious experience of God.

My own reading of the mystics in this book was that kind of search for a vicarious experience of God. As with Holy Scripture, in reading the mystics I feel that God is somehow there in the words. God created everything with words, and so through words I hope to be recreated.

For those in the Judeo-Christian tradition, no mystical writing incarnates the divine power and presence as does the Bible. Within that same tradition, no other book has more often been prostituted for purposes other than those for which it was intended. It has been used as a scientific treatise, a political weapon, a substitute for a liberal education, a justification for anything from an unjust war to the death penalty to the exclusion of those who are of a different point of view or philosophy. God's word has been used throughout history to confirm and validate human words, becoming a verbal tower of Babel that divides rather than unites us in God.

No other Judeo-Christian text demands more of the reader because it demands the humility to listen to God, not our own prejudices. The Bible, in short, demands that we abdicate our need to be gods. The Bible's truth is that God alone is God; God alone is. God is God, and we are but creatures dependent on God for everything yet endowed by God with a free will that can reject God's primacy, privileging our will over God's will.

Cardinal John Henry Newman once said that one can tell whose words are important to a preacher by the way he proclaims the Scriptures and the way he preaches. Which words does he proclaim more effectively?

Without God's sustaining love we are nothing. God alone keeps us in existence. Once we realize that, we want to know more about this God. Who is God, and what does God have to do with us? That is *the* question, and so we go in search of words and other signs that can reveal to us who God is and, thereby, who we are.

Thus, after Scripture and nature, we turn to the mystics. What has God revealed to them? Anything more or other than is in Scripture? Anything more than is revealed in the Word that is Jesus Christ? I have not found in the mystics anything more than God has revealed in Christ—at least not anything more that relates to the question, "Who is God, and what does God have to do with us?"

Why, then, read the mystics at all? I do because in the mystics I see God speaking and relating with humans in their own language throughout the ages. In every age down to our own, God speaks to individual men and women just as God spoke to Abraham and Moses and the prophets.

God is not dead; God continues to be involved with all of creation and to speak with human beings as intimates. What is more, in the language of the mystics, in their metaphors and images, we see revealed the intimate union we all have with God, an intimacy as close as the love expressed in the Song of Songs. We see the profound transformation that happens in people once they realize in a tangible way who God is and who God is in relation to us.

As in times past, God speaks to individuals, and they are transformed. We, in turn, are transformed by their stories when we recognize that their stories are our stories, too. The mystics see and act upon the truth about all of us. If we but see in faith what they see, in fact, we, too, experience the effects of God's power and presence in our lives. The mystics show us by their visions and lives that what our faith attests and theology teaches is indeed true: God is, and God is intimately involved with us today and always.

It took a long time and a lot of painful mistakes for me to understand that mystics need to be read within the context of their own times. They can be trusted in some things but can also be tainted at times with less than healthy attitudes, such as an anti-Incarnational fear of the body or of sexuality, a denigrating view of the material world as a necessary evil or simply as a passageway to the spirit. These kinds of dichotomies, splitting matter and spirit, body and soul, if not a part of a mystic's pure vision, can be a part of how the mystic relates his or her experience. The mystics' attitudes become the lens through which the world is seen.

Even if the mystic's own vision is pure, a narrator or translator can be so much a child of his or her own times that a modern reader finds the stories bizarre or even dangerous. Madness is something I feared, as a young man, would result from my reading and trying to imitate the visions and lives of the mystics. I was attracted to mystical literature but also afraid of it and for a time opted for the "safer" course of biblical literature.

Holy Scripture has the sanction of the church as the Word of God written down by human beings whose words were inspired by God. The extra-biblical mystics, as attractive as they are, need to be read with great caution and intelligent discernment. The same could be said of Scripture, of course, but in the Catholic tradition, the church sanctions the interpretation and determines how Scripture is to be read and what it means. Private revelation does not have the weight of divine revelation. Private revelations can be helpful and inspirational, but they are not necessary to one's faith.

The mystics have been touched by God in an extraordinary way and in some cases have written extraordinarily well of the inner journey. Every mystical text is the story of an individual's encounter with God. In those words we can find inspiration and motivation to seek, with the same single-minded perseverance, to be open to God's voice.

Not every mystic will appeal to everyone, but one or the other may strike a chord in the heart of someone trying to live the Gospel and know God. Something you read will speak to you, and you will say, "This is the saint for me; I believe this; I trust these words, this life."

chapter one

MARY, MOTHER OF MYSTICS

If the mystic is one who experiences in an extraordinary way the intimacy with God offered to everyone, then Mary is the model and pattern of the mystical life. She literally carried God in her womb and gave birth to him.

Spiritual impregnation, gestation and giving birth are the initial stages of the mystical life. God invades our life, usually when we are not expecting it; we embrace that gift. Even if we are tempted to hoard it as ours alone, God will be born from us; we will serve others as a result of God's own indwelling love.

Imagine Mary, a young girl at her prayers or perhaps performing her tasks or simply sitting and watching people pass by her window. Suddenly, there is a rush of wind like a flutter of wings, or a flash of light, and there is one like an angel addressing her: "Greetings, favored one! The Lord is with you" (Luke 1:28). There it is: The Lord is with you. What can this mean? Gabriel, as if knowing her thoughts, continues, "Do not be afraid, Mary, for you have found favor with God. And now, you will conceive in your womb and bear a son, and you will name him Jesus" (Luke 1:30–31).

Mary asks, "How can this be, since I am a virgin?" "The Holy Spirit will come upon you, and the power of the Most High will over-shadow you…" (Luke 1:34–35).

All mystics wonder what is happening to them when the Holy Spirit asks them to believe the seemingly impossible, that God wants to enter their lives. They can, of course, refuse out of fear or doubt, and it is the glory of Mary that she does not refuse but says yes.

Each true mystic who says yes to God at some point sends forth into the world as the Father sent the Son to announce and build up God's kingdom. For Mary this moment comes almost immediately when the angel announces that her aged cousin Elizabeth is in her sixth month of pregnancy (for nothing is impossible with God). Mary says to the angel, "Here I am, the servant of the Lord; let it be with me according to your word" (Luke 1:38).

And Mary sets out into the hill country to minister to her cousin Elizabeth. There God will be revealed in Mary's deep charity, as God had been revealed in her deep prayer. For when she enters Elizabeth's house, the baby in Elizabeth's womb leaps, and Elizabeth, filled with the Holy Spirit, cries out, "Blessed are you among women, and blessed is the fruit of your womb…. And blessed is she who believed that there would be a fulfillment of what was spoken to her by the Lord" (Luke 1:42, 45).

Mary's decision and the truth of the angel's message is confirmed, not when Mary is rapt in contemplation, but when she is doing charity. The truth of the mystic's visions and intimacy with God is proven in the selfless charity of the mystic's life.

Mary's response to Elizabeth, her canticle, the Magnificat, distills the mystical life:

My soul magnifies the Lord,

and my spirit rejoices in God my Savior,

for he has looked with favor on the lowliness of his servant.

Surely, from now on all generations will call me blessed;

for the Mighty One has done great things for me

and holy is his name.

His mercy is for those who fear him

from generation to generation.

He has shown strength with his arm;

he has scattered the proud in the thoughts of their hearts.

He has brought down the powerful from their thrones,

and lifted up the lowly;

he has filled the hungry with good things,

and sent the rich away empty.

He has helped his servant Israel,

in remembrance of his mercy,

according to the promise he made to our ancestors,

to Abraham and his descendants for ever. (Luke 1:46–55)

As with every true prayer, the Magnificat does just that: it *magnifies* the Lord, focuses on the Almighty, who does great things among us, the One whose name is holy.

As though already letting the child in her womb speak through her, Mary does more: She presages the major themes of Jesus' future preaching and ministry. William Barclay, in his meditations on the Gospel of Luke, says that Mary ends her canticle with a moral, social and economic revolution.[1]

The moral revolution is indicated in the line that God "scatters the proud in the plans of their hearts" (in Barclay's translation). We begin to change when our own plans scatter us, bring us down; God's plans replace them—God's plans, in the case of the mystic, are revealed in a vision or a voice speaking to the soul. God's plans work a revolution in our lives. We begin to change because of what we have seen and heard.

The social revolution is heralded in the line, "He has brought down the powerful from their thrones / and lifted up the lowly." The mystic sees what the world does not see, that the lowly are the real authority, for they represent the kingdom of God in its fullness.

Jesus says in the first words of his first sermon, "Blessed are the poor in spirit, for theirs is the kingdom of heaven" (Matthew 5:3). Jesus does not say, "Theirs *will* be the kingdom of heaven," but "Theirs *is* the kingdom of heaven." This is a *now* promise. Where there is poverty of spirit, the real kingdom happens. How different this is from the kingdoms of earth that happen where there is power, not lowliness and littleness. How powerless the mystics are in terms of human power, how powerful in things of the spiritual kingdom within.

The economic revolution is foretold when Mary says, "[H]e has filled the hungry with good things, / and sent the rich away empty." The kingdom Jesus will preach and that his disciples will model distributes wealth to the poor, embracing poverty as the fast track into the kingdom. "If you wish to be perfect," Jesus says to the rich, young man, "go, sell your possessions, and give the money to the poor, and you will have treasure in heaven; then come, follow me" (Matthew 19:21). The medieval mystic Francis of Assisi will become the personification of this kind of gospel poverty, having been a rich young man who knew all too well that it is "easier for a camel to go through the eye of a needle than for someone who is rich to enter the kingdom of God" (Matthew 19:24).

Mary's life, like that of her son, will be a living out of her own canticle. She will enter into the mysteries of Christ's life. Like the Christian mystics after her, she will participate in a more intense way in the very mystery that she is sharing. As the model of intimacy with God, Mary will enter into the death and resurrection of her son. She will stand beneath the cross of his dying; she will rise with him body and soul in the mystery of her Assumption into heaven.

Franciscans pray a seven-decade rosary, the Franciscan Crown, that for me summarizes what it means to enter into the mystery of how we are transformed by and into Christ. The mystic knows in a uniquely graced way these mysteries that we believe and live out as we try to be true to the mystery of our baptism.

The very word *mystic* derives from the word *mystery*, and God does allow the mystics to see into mysteries, like the mystery of baptism, by way of visions or insights that transcend our usual way of seeing. They see and relate to us the wonder of what is happening within us, for example, as we live out the mysteries of our salvation. The mystics confirm that what we believe is indeed true.

The seven joys of Mary of the Franciscan Crown illustrate for me what happens in the lives of mystics.

1. *Annunciation*. Like Mary, the mystics have experienced some extraordinary visitation of God. They hear or see Christ or his messenger, and they are given a choice to respond or not. They realize that their experience of the Divine not only involves listening, but responding.

2. *Visitation*. The response to God's annunciation ultimately involves a reaching out to others, as Mary does in the second mystery of the crown, the Visitation. When she hears of her cousin Elizabeth's pregnancy, Mary goes immediately to tend to her, to be her handmaid. She becomes her cousin's servant as she became God's servant in the Annunciation. The one leads to the other, and, indeed, to be handmaid to her cousin is to be handmaid to God. For, as her son will proclaim, when you serve the least of your brothers and sisters, you serve him.

3. *Nativity*. The mystical heart gives birth to God in poverty, littleness and often in obscurity. Mystics do not literally give birth to Christ, but they do so spiritually by their charity, by the gestures of their lives.

4. *Adoration of the Magi*. The mystics imitate the adoration of the magi symbolically and literally when they offer their newborn selves to God. They have a sense that they no longer belong wholly to themselves to do with their lives as they please, but they belong to God.

5. *Finding Jesus in the Temple*. The finding of the child Jesus in the temple speaks to the truth not only of the mystic's life but of all our lives, namely, that we can't hold onto God. God will be about God's business, and nothing we do will make God our personal possession.

We all experience this one way or another, but the mystics experience this most intensely because of the felt intimacy with God they've been gifted with. God at some point withdraws his presence, and the mystic is left in that dark night of soul, to use the language of John of the Cross, in which God seems to no longer exist, at least not for them. They long to experience God, but they cannot make it happen, because God is leading them through this dark night in order that they might love God for God's own sake and not for the intimacy and gifts God gives them. And so they wait, and they go through the motions of prayer and charity; but there is no consolation, no joy in it, until God finds them again, and their joy is restored to a heart that has been purified of selfishness.

6. *Resurrection.* Jesus' resurrection is prefigured by the transfiguration. When Jesus takes Peter, James and John up the mountain and is transfigured before them, they try to hold onto that experience the way other mystics have tried to hold onto their ecstatic experience of God. Jesus' face is changed, and his clothing becomes dazzling white, and Moses and Elijah appear in glory, speaking of the passage Jesus will have to make in Jerusalem. Peter immediately wants to make three shelters there for Jesus, Moses and Elijah in order to keep them there. But the evangelist Luke says that Peter doesn't know what he is saying because, as he is speaking, a cloud comes and covers them with a shadow, and the disciples are afraid. Then a voice comes from the cloud, "This is my Son, my Chosen; listen to him!" (Luke 9:35). Jesus is left standing there alone. The vision has passed, and shortly afterward Jesus enters Jerusalem, beginning his passion, death and resurrection.

15

We, not even Mary, can hold onto glory. The ordinary passages through life and death continue as they did for Mary after meeting her son as the Risen Lord following the Resurrection. The mystic, however, has indeed seen the vision, has heard God's voice. Those of us who have not are encouraged by their visions and voices to believe more firmly that beneath the appearances of our ordinary lives God's glory lies hidden. It flares out from time to time and is seen by those to whom God chooses to reveal this parallel world we believe in but do not see.

7. *Assumption and Crowning of Mary.* Like Mary in this last mystery, the mystics are assumed into heaven soul and body. By this I mean that only in the integration of soul and body do we enter paradise. Once one has had an intense experience of God, the temptation is to privilege the soul and denigrate the body, thereby splitting what God has made one person. Some mystics have seen the body as a problem, a source of sin, an inferior part of the self, and they have acted accordingly, often imposing extreme penances on the body, neglecting the needs of the body, even trying to become pure soul. This is another form of trying to hold onto God. Instead we must let God go, as Mary did when she saw her son die, saw him alive again, then saw him ascend into heaven. Following Jesus' instructions, she went with John to his home on Patmos to live out her days.

There is a beautiful poem by the English poet Anne Beresford that in its simple, homely gestures speaks beautifully of Mary, the integrated woman as seen through the eyes of Saint John.

On Patmos

In the beginning
silence
her hands cold
she would stroke my face
and murmur thanks

We share peace
on this island

My memories, visions
written down.
Work assigned to me
when Peter asked:
"And what of him?"

My mother of the Word
Sits in the centre of the universe
slowly dying into her thoughts.[2]

Here is Mary, the aging woman, not Mary, pure soul.

The coronation of Mary as queen of heaven and earth speaks to the truth of our relationship with God. Our coronation comes in the marriage of the soul to God, which the mystics experience in an ecstatic state, and which some of the mystics wrote about, as we will see in the pages that follow.

One misconception about the mystics is that they are singularly holy people, set apart from us ordinary Christians by their holiness.

Nothing could be further from the truth. Mystics are singular and different because of their mystical experiences, their visions, not their holiness. Holiness is about living in the grace of God, about virtue, especially the virtue of charity, which is available to all; it is not about visions. Jesus says that there is no greater love than to lay down one's life for one's friends. Peter, James and John are not holier than the other apostles because they saw Jesus transfigured; they are only different because they've had an experience the other apostles didn't have. They knew something more than the others.

Holiness is about faith, not knowledge. Holiness is about abiding in faith, hope and charity. And such is available to everyone open to the Holy Spirit.

Another misconception is that the mystics are special friends of God, and the rest of us are not. Again, that is not true. We are all special friends of God if we keep God's commandments. What is unique about the mystics is the revelations they receive. That makes them distinctive persons in the Body of Christ, but no more necessary. As Saint Paul says, there are many gifts of the Spirit, but the most important, and the only essential one, is the one available to all: charity. "Love never ends," he says. "But as for prophecies, they will come to an end; as for tongues, they will cease; as for knowledge, it will come to an end" (1 Corinthians 13:8).

How, then, are these mysteries we believe and that the mystics have glimpsed lived out from day to day? Let's imagine the Gospel stories as a series of scenes of which we ourselves are a part.

Mary and Joseph take Jesus to Jerusalem to present him to the Lord. Simeon is there waiting for the fulfillment of the Holy Spirit's promise to him that he would not die before he had seen the Lord's Messiah. And Mary knows, as soon as she sees him that he, too, is of the fellowship of the Holy Spirit that overshadowed her. He is aflame with a fire she recognizes as he takes the child Jesus in his arms and begins to praise God, saying,

> Master, now you are dismissing your servant in peace,
>> according to your word;
> for my eyes have seen your salvation,
>> which you have prepared in the presence of all peoples,
> a light for revelation to the Gentiles
> and for glory to your people Israel. (Luke 2:29–32)

Mary and Joseph marvel that once again someone knows who their son is beneath all that littleness, that baby smile, those tiny, round cheeks. Mary is not prepared for what comes next as Simeon turns his eyes to her and the inspired words flow out from his aged body: "This child is destined for the falling and rising of many in Israel, and to be a sign that will be opposed so that the inner thoughts of many will be revealed—and a sword will pierce your own soul too" (Luke 2:34–35).

Like the mystics after her, Mary's glory and joy are also her suffering. A chill runs through her, not so much for herself as for her son, and the words of Isaiah sweep over her like an angry wind threatening the helpless baby in her arms:

> I gave my back to those who struck me,
>> and my cheeks to those who pulled out the beard;
> I did not hide my face
>> from insult and spitting. (Isaiah 50:6)

Already she feels the sword, and she shudders. Then the prophetess Anna comes in just at that moment and begins to prophesy about Mary's child to everyone looking forward to the redemption of Israel. The dark wind passes and they return to Nazareth like the mystics who, having experienced great light and darkness, return to their ordinary lives.

Then Joseph hears terrible news in a dream and sweeps them away into Egypt. King Herod is also searching for the child, not enlightened by the Holy Spirit, but made aware of this king's birth by the Magi, who went looking for the newborn king at King Herod's court—a newborn king, an ominous threat to Herod's throne. He must destroy him lest these astrologers prove right and a new king is already there among them.

So Joseph, Mary's husband, the man of dreams, learns from an angel in a dream, as he had learned from another angel in a dream that Mary's pregnancy, her disgrace, is really grace, because what has been conceived in her is of the Holy Spirit. And he believed and became like her and Elizabeth and the Magi, like Simeon and Anna, one of those of the Holy Spirit. Thus, heeding the angel's warning to flee into Egypt and stay there until the angel tells them otherwise, Joseph and Mary take the child and go into Egypt, reversing Israel's long forty-year passage from Egypt, through the desert, into the Holy Land of promise.

Again, Mary the mystic experiences the reversal of the way. Where she thought they were going is suddenly reversed, and the cold, dark wind of Simeon's prophecy chills the night air into Egypt. But Mary believes this return to Egypt is of the Holy Spirit because an angel,

God's messenger, has directed them to go for the safety of her child who, though he is worthy of worship, is still a little baby, vulnerable, unable to speak, dependent on her and Joseph's care. What mystery is here, that Divinity and humanity are so conjoined! And why is it that Israel must now return to Egypt? What sign is this? What symbol is here so darkly given?

No dream is perfect, no way the only way, no direction irreversible by God, whose way is the way of reversal, as Mary's son soon will make clear when he leaves her and Joseph in the lurch at the age of twelve and does not accompany them home to Nazareth from Jerusalem. So Mary makes her way, another reversal, back to Jerusalem, where she and Joseph search anxiously among the crowds there for Passover, looking for their lost son.

However, as they soon discover, he is not lost. He has, at twelve years of age, found himself. They find him in the temple teaching. Mary is hurt by this unexpected reversal, this atypical behavior from so perfect a son who had been growing in grace and wisdom; she feels her own son wielding the sword that is piercing her heart.

And she says as much. "Child, why have you treated us like this? Look, your father and I have been searching for you in great anxiety" (Luke 2:48). Jesus' response must have been hurtful to Joseph, who was already painfully aware of how little he had to do with the conception and birth of this child: "Did you not know that I must be in my Father's house?" (Luke 2:49). The implication hits so hard—my *real* father, the one who matters, the God of Abraham. Joseph now gives back God's gift, Joseph the mystic, who has known the revelation of dreams and angels.

Mary must hurt for Joseph, but they both understand that the Holy Spirit has once again surfaced, this time painfully, their own small roles clearly evident in this huge story of God's prophecies coming to pass. Their road suddenly shrinks; their way seems poor compared to *the* way, who is this very boy, so good and obedient and kind who now, like Joseph and Mary before him, has heard the Spirit's call and recognizes that voice and suddenly begins to remember who he is, dimly, but certainly; no other voice will have the same power over him as this voice, the echo of his own. It is as if his own voice is calling him, yet it is the Holy Spirit. They somehow are one.

Mary and Joseph in humility and love begin to recede into the background, Joseph forever, and Mary emerging only briefly throughout her son's life on earth.

Jesus is so much a part of Mary and yet so separate, so other. She watches him grow away and then go away to follow the same Spirit she had followed leaving her parents' home in Nazareth to begin her own way, God's way, following the Spirit and then her son all the way to Calvary, emerging in his story only twice: once in Cana in Galilee and once when she waits outside to see him as he proclaimed the Spirit's words.

At Cana it is she who hears the Holy Spirit and is moved to nudge Jesus into his ministry of miracles. It is time. There is a wedding at Cana, and she is there, as is he, her son now grown beyond her imagining when he lay a tiny baby at her breast. The host has run out of wine, and she knows in the Spirit that Jesus must begin his miraculous ministry with water and wine, as he would end it with blood and wine.

"They have no wine," she says to him. And he to her, "Woman, what concern is that to you and to me? My hour has not yet come" (John 2:3, 4).

But it has, and so she says uncharacteristically, "Do whatever he tells you" (John 2:5). And he changes the water into fine wine, as later he will change the wine into his blood poured out and consumed by those who share the Spirit's table with him.

She speaks beyond herself, her knowing, as do all those who live in the Spirit. She speaks in the Spirit, as Jesus will later speak in the Spirit when she and his brothers wait outside to speak to him. "Look, your mother and your brothers are standing outside, wanting to speak to you" (Matthew 12:47).

Always, it seems, she is outside now, following him on the road, waiting to catch a glimpse of him, to hear him speak, see for herself what manner of man the Holy Spirit has fashioned. Immediately she hears and receives her answer. Pointing to his disciples, he says, "Here are my mother and my brothers! For whoever does the will of my Father in heaven is my brother and sister and mother" (Matthew 12:49–50). And now she knows. He has moved at last into that other world beneath and within all things that is his kingdom, that *more*, which is the presence of God revealed to us in the Spirit. And she knows, or thinks she knows, that her work is complete.

One who does the will of my Father in heaven is my sister and mother. An apt description of Mary herself. Does she, in hearing his words to her that day, know he is painting his perfect disciple in the image of her? Does she know that he knows how perfectly she has kept God's commandments? Does she know that all those who bear Christ in their hearts and give him birth anew will be doing so in imitation of her? If

23

she does, she knows in the same Spirit who is speaking through him; if she doesn't know, then she will later when, from the cross, Jesus entrusts his own adopted "son" to her, the youngest disciple, John.

"Woman, here is your son." Then he will say to the disciple, " 'Here is your mother.' And from that hour the disciple will take her into his own home" (John 19:26, 27). The "perfect" apostle is the child of Mary. She is the model, the one who brings forth the Son of God, the Head of the Mystical Body; she is the one who brings to birth in the same Spirit the members of that Body.

After the terrible dark night of Calvary and the light of Pentecost when she waits with the disciples, she makes the passage to Patmos with John where he sees her in the Holy Spirit, she who lives daily, simply, with him. Suddenly she emerges powerfully in his visions as a "woman clothed with the sun, with the moon under her feet, and on her head a crown of twelve stars" (Revelation 12:1). This is the same woman, much older now, who sits with him daily and prays with him and shares his life.

There is left only the final passage validating all the others, when, falling into the deep sleep of her thoughts, she is assumed body and soul into heaven, the eternal mother of the new heaven and the new earth, which John sees in one of his final visions: "Then I saw a new heaven and a new earth; for the first heaven and the first earth had passed away, and the sea was no more. And I saw the holy city, the new Jerusalem, coming down out of heaven from God, prepared as a bride adorned for her husband" (Revelation 21:1–2).

The life of Mary is a template one could place over every mystic: an Annunciation of the Spirit, a giving birth to God, a sense of the

Incarnate God's presence, and following the life of the God who is human from Nazareth to Calvary to his Resurrection and Ascension to the return of the Spirit at Pentecost. And all the time in between is Ordinary Time, in which one incarnates God in one's own daily life, nurturing God and sharing God with others. The whole journey is summed up in Mary's words, "Here am I, the servant of the Lord; let it be with me according to your word" (Luke 1:38).

---

reflection

"'The first man, Adam, became a living being,' the last Adam became a life-giving spirit." (1 Corinthians 15:45)

As I sat with Mary listening to her mystical journey, I was led inevitably to her Son, Jesus Christ. It struck me that it is the Christ who is a life-giving Spirit who informs the church. The historical Christ is our model, but the proof of the Incarnation of God is the life-giving Spirit, the Risen Lord, the cosmic and simultaneously indwelling Christ.

To concentrate exclusively on the historical Christ is to impoverish the mystery of the Incarnation, just as to focus wholly on the Risen life-giving Lord can lead to a kind of spiritualism that eschews the physical. As Saint Paul writes of Adam and Christ, "Just as we have borne the image of the man of dust, we will also bear the image of the man of heaven" (1 Corinthians 15:49).

Incarnation and transformation, death and resurrection, Ascending Lord and Descending Spirit: These are the dimensions and parameters of our life in God made tangible for us in the life of Jesus

Christ. Again, Saint Paul: "But it is not the spiritual that is first, but the physical, and then the spiritual" (1 Corinthians 15:46).

In order to understand the historical Christ, one must have knowledge of the times and of the genres and the making of the books of the New Testament; in order to know the Risen, Cosmic Christ, one must participate of the same Spirit, who is the wisdom of God. The Christ of history requires learning; the Risen Christ, revelation and vision and faith. The historical and human requires human knowing, the cosmic, divine. These two ways of knowing complement one another, but it is the latter which gives life and transforms the human, thereby revealing the life-giving Spirit, who informs everything that is.

Any deep and complete reading of Scripture, therefore, must be informed by human knowledge of the history and nature of the individual books of the Bible and also the book of the Bible as a whole. It must also be a reading informed by the Holy Spirit and the discernment of the church that is the work of the same Spirit, who first descended on the apostles and those with them on Pentecost, the Spirit who was subsequently given to those who heard the apostles preach in the same Spirit on Pentecost, thus becoming church, an inspirited community of believers sharing the same Spirit throughout the ages.

chapter two

FRANCIS OF ASSISI, THE PRACTICAL MYSTIC (1182–1226)

The pigeons are gathering already, though it's only 11:00 AM, a propitious time in the Piazza del Comune. The gathering of pigeons signals the approaching noon feeding time. When the bells in the medieval town begin to ring, hundreds of pigeons will strut and rise in short flights. Children will delight and some will be frightened as their parents lead them into the carpet of birds feeding in front of the Temple of Minerva. Noontime in Assisi.

Much of the city is there in that noontime ritual: the birds and the children, the onlooking tourists and natives who sit at the outdoor tables that front the nearby bars. A procession of tourists or pilgrims walks around or through the pigeons, and I am reminded of Saint Francis and the birds: a good reason to lose myself in the scene and remember where I am. This is the birthplace of Francesco Bernardone, whom the world knows as Saint Francis of Assisi. *Of Assisi*, a phrase that defines much of who he is and the unique way he lived his extraordinary life.

Today the sun is blinding as I look up from my cappuccino and see the pigeons strutting nervously as they wait for noon, and at the other end of the piazza the fountain where Francis and his first companion, Bernard of Quintavalle, in a lavish gesture, gave away all of Bernard's possessions, thus signaling the beginning of Bernard's life as a poor penitent Brother of Assisi.

Of Assisi. At that time Assisi was a city divided geographically between nobles (the *majores*, the greater ones) and merchants and the poor (the *minores*, the lesser ones). The towered homes of the nobles rose high in the upper part of the city, while the poor lived in lower Assisi, and the merchants in between. Upper and lower were divided, generally speaking, by the Piazza del Comune, the main piazza of the city. Rival families lived in constant tension in anticipation of the next brawl or outright battle between their houses. As a boy and young man, Francis saw these divisions and this omnipresent hostility and quarreling. War was a reality that ran through Francis' years as a river of blood.

This was his Assisi, as were the interminable conflicts between the supporters of the pope and the emperor, the papal Guelfs and imperial Ghibellines, whose struggles for supremacy tore apart city after city and divided one city from another, their walled fortress-like towns a now-dumb tribute to the clamor of their dissensions.

I leave the pigeons and the fountain and walk toward the Piazza of Saint Clare from where I will be able to see Assisi's own walled fortress, the Rocca Maggiore, the symbol of the emperor's power over Assisi and the surrounding countryside. The Rocca Maggiore and all the violence it symbolizes prepares Francis for knighthood and war, and to war he does go, only to be captured in the first battle at Ponte

San Giovanni between Assisi and her rival, Perugia. Capture and prison and a year of illness after he is finally released lay the groundwork for the inner journey, just as violence and war precipitate the young Francis' outer journey, which he resumes as soon as he is well. But only a day's journey out of Assisi, Francis experiences the first of his dreams and voices that change him utterly. The mystic journey begins.

But I am ahead of myself, still looking up at the Rocca Maggiore, at those heights Francis longed to attain. He would instead descend from those heights again and again before he finally ascended the mountain of God, La Verna, and met there the Six-Winged Seraph with the body of a crucified man—all of which is yet to come. He has yet to be born and live. Of that story these are the bare outlines that we will flesh out as we explore Francis' mysticism.

Francesco Bernardone was born in 1182 in the Umbrian town of Assisi and was baptized John. At the time of his baptism his father was away on a business trip to France; when he returned, he changed his son's name to Francesco, "the Frenchman."

True to his nickname, the boy grew up enamored of the French language and of the tales of the knights and ladies of French Romance. He was a carefree, generous young man who pursued the good life with gusto, partying and carousing with his friends. But throughout all the levity of his younger years, he dreamed of becoming a knight—a serious, bloody enterprise. And when a war broke out between Assisi and its neighbor, Perugia, he got his chance to ride off to war as a knight of Assisi, only to be captured as a prisoner of war in the defeat of Assisi in the very first skirmish.

How could he have known that this was the end of war for him, this humiliating defeat of his hometown? How could he have known that the year of imprisonment in a Perugian prison would change him deeply? And he, but twenty-one years old, returning home to Assisi a broken man, to lie in bed for a year. A year in prison, a year in bed. He, the richest young man in Assisi, a man his companions had dubbed "King of the Revels," Francis, the son of the cloth merchant Pietro Bernardone and the Frenchwoman Lady Pica.

He would try to go to war again as a knight in the papal army battling the forces of the Holy Roman Emperor, but God had other plans and in a vision told Francis to return to Assisi where it would be revealed to him what he was to do. And so Francis retreated from war, and one day while he was praying before the crucifix of the dilapidated little chapel of San Damiano, outside the walls of Assisi, he received his call from God. From the crucifix came the voice, "Francis, go and rebuild my house which, as you see, is falling utterly to ruin."[1]

Francis was to build, to repair, not to tear down with weapons of destruction. He began to beg for stones and repaired with his own hands the run-down chapel of San Damiano, which was the "house" Francis believed his vision referred to. It was this house, this little church, but it was more. It was the larger house, the Catholic church itself, that he was to repair.

Francis learned this larger implication of the vision one day when he saw a leper on the road and impulsively jumped from his horse, gave coins to the leper and embraced him. Unbelievably, he was not repulsed, but filled with joy, for he realized he had embraced his Lord, Jesus Christ.

That is how it happened that Francis went to live among the lepers, ministering to them and learning from them. There, he realized, were the living stones, and together, they were building the kingdom of God on earth. There was God among the rejected, the despised, the poor.

Thus it began, the Franciscan rebuilding of the church. Others soon joined Francis, and they became a brotherhood, and the church approved their way of life: to live with the poor as poor men who observed the holy gospel wholeheartedly.

Francis and the brothers preached and worked with their hands for their daily bread, and when they received nothing for their labor, they begged for their food. They continued to live among the lepers, making peace with them and with all people and all creation by making peace with their own aversion to the lepers. They embraced them instead of running away.

Women came to join them; the first was Clare, the daughter of the knight Favarone di Offreduccio. The bishop of Assisi gave Clare and her companions as their cloister San Damiano, the church Francis himself had restored with his own hands. There they lived in extreme gospel poverty in contemplation of the Poor Crucified Christ. They worked with their hands and depended on the begging of the brothers for their sustenance. They prayed for and ministered to the sick who were brought to their door.

Francis, in the meantime, was expanding the brothers' ministry beyond Assisi to all of Italy and even farther. He himself, with one or two brothers, made missionary journeys preaching conversion and forgiveness, which he saw as *the* means of peacemaking. He traveled to

Spain, France, Switzerland, Dalmatia and even to Syria, the Holy Land and Egypt during the Fifth Crusade. He tried to be a peacemaker between Christians and Muslims, going so far as to enter the camp of the sultan, again preaching conversion of heart and forgiveness; the sultan listened and gave Francis safe passage through his kingdom.

The animal and plant worlds, too, received Francis' compassionate love. He reached out to and reverenced all created things. He preached to the animals and birds and fish. He embraced and tamed the ravening wolf of Gubbio.

He preached always the God-man, Jesus Christ, and tried to make him visible and tangible, as when, three years before his death, he celebrated Midnight Mass with live animals to re-create the first Christmas, thus popularizing the tradition of the Christmas crib.

The following year, while Francis was in deep prayer on the mountain of La Verna in Tuscany, he received the sacred stigmata, the five wounds of Christ, becoming himself a visible image of his crucified Lord.

Shortly afterward he sang his "Canticle of the Creatures," the swan song that summed up his life and attested to the peace and joy and integration a life of love and forgiveness brings. He sang of all creatures as his brothers and sisters and bade them forgive one another if they wished to be crowned by God. He then welcomed even death as his sister and embraced her.

The man who longed to be a knight, a man of war, died a man of peace—at peace with God, with himself and with all of creation. God changed his heart, and his changed heart changed the world.

The mysticism of Saint Francis grew out of and was not separate from his Catholic sacramental and gospel life. Francis' intimacy with God was not a category of experience separate from his intense living of the gospel within the Catholic church.

True, at the beginning, when he was still "in the world," as he put it, he was gifted with ecstatic dreams and with the vision of Christ speaking to him from the crucifix of San Damiano and with the vision of Christ the Leper. But even then Francis did not have these visions and dreams in order to draw him into himself but to draw him into the mystery of the church. "Go and rebuild my house," the voice of the crucifix spoke, "which, as you see, is falling utterly to ruin." Francis went out and begged for stones to repair the ramshackle chapel of San Damiano, and eventually the house of the larger church itself. And when he saw Christ in a leper, Francis went to live among the lepers. "[A]nd the Lord Himself led me among them," Francis writes in his Testament, "and I worked mercy with them."[2]

The visitations from the Lord led Francis into church-building and church-making together with others, not into self-absorption. In the same way, the inner conversions he experienced and his lifelong walking in the footsteps of the poor Christ derived from his response to the Gospel on two occasions, especially, in February and April of 1208.

The first occasion was the Gospel Reading on the Feast of Saint Matthias, February 24. After Mass Francis, who'd been moved by the reading, asked the priest to explain the gospel to him, which the priest did, line by line. When he heard the words that Christ's true disciples should "Take no gold, or silver, or copper in their belts, no bag for your journey, or two tunics, or sandals, or a staff" (Matthew 10:9–10),

Francis was filled with joy and cried out, "This is what I want; this is what I desire with all my heart!"[3] Francis began immediately to live out Christ's words.

This is Francis the practical mystic, one who responded whole-heartedly to God's Word and in that response God was revealed. Everyone can be this kind of mystic with God's grace. The practical mystic is not one with secret knowledge of God, but one who knows God in doing the will of God.

Francis expands on this practical mysticism for everyone when he writes in his "Letter to the Faithful,"

> We are his bride when our faithful soul is united with Jesus Christ by the Holy Spirit; we are his brothers and sisters when we do the will of his Father who is in heaven, and we are mother to him when we carry him in our hearts and souls through love and a pure and sincere conscience, and give him birth by doing good.[4]

This is a mysticism for everyone. This is a mysticism Francis offers to all believers, a mysticism which he illustrates through the gestures of his own life. The Franciscan mystic is the ordinary Christian mystic who is brother, sister, bride and mother of Christ by means of a fidelity, made possible by the Holy Spirit, in doing God's will, in carrying Christ within and through love and a pure and sincere conscience and in giving birth to Christ by the charity of good works. In all of this is intimacy with God, and intimacy with God that results in charity is practical mysticism.

It is interesting that Francis' response takes place within a liturgical setting and that he seeks the explanation of the priest before he acts on God's Word. His personal response to the Gospel had begun, and it was precipitated by hearing the Gospel read at Mass.

On April 16 of that same year, Francis was approached by the son of a wealthy nobleman of Assisi, Bernard of Quintavalle, about how Bernard might "reject the world" after the example of Francis, who answered that they needed to seek God's counsel. The two then went to the church of Saint Nicholas in Assisi, and after they'd prayed, Francis opened the Missal three times to discern God's will.

The first text to appear was: "If you wish to be perfect, go, sell your possessions, and give the money to the poor" (Matthew 19:21). The second read: "Take nothing for your journey" (Luke 9:3). And the third, "If any want to become my followers, let them deny themselves and take up their cross and follow me" (Matthew 16:24). And Francis said, "This is our life and rule, and that of all who wish to join our company."5

Again it is the Word of God in the liturgical Mass book that Francis and Bernard consult, and what the three openings reveal become their rule of life, not just for Bernard and Francis, but for all who will join them. When the revelation Francis received on the Feast of Saint Matthias was confirmed by Bernard's joining him, he envisioned a company of those who, like him and Bernard, would live out this scriptural rule of life. Within the parameters of that rule and in the church, which was to confirm it officially in the person of Pope Innocent III, Francis and others who joined that holy enterprise experienced profound intimacy with God through transformation into Christ.

The most dramatic visual confirmation of that intimacy was revealed in the very flesh of Francis himself in the sacred stigmata he received on Mount La Verna in September of 1224, two years before he died and sixteen years after Francis and Bernard embraced the way of life revealed to them in the opening of the Missal.

It was an experience revealed within the brotherhood and in the community that is the church as Francis was in retreat to prepare for the Feast of Saint Michael the Archangel. As the life of the brothers was an intensification of the life lived by all Christians, so Francis' life was an intensification of the gospel life the brothers lived in common.

The sacred stigmata is the dramatic visual representation of Francis as the personification of one "wounded" by God's word as described in the Letter to the Hebrews: "Indeed, the word of God is living and active, sharper than any two-edged sword, piercing until it divides soul from spirit, joints from marrow..." (Hebrews 4:12). And again in Isaiah: My word "shall not return to me empty, / but it shall accomplish that which I purpose, / and succeed in the thing for which I sent it" (Isaiah 55:11).

All the mystics fulfill these words, of course, but there is something swift and dramatic in the way Saint Francis responds to God's word. He hears the word of God, and he carries it out without reservation, without counting the cost, without equivocation.

"Go and repair my house which, as you see, is falling into ruin," the voice from the San Damiano crucifix entreats; Francis goes out and rushes to his father's shop, takes a bolt of the best cloth, mounts one of his father's fine steeds and rides to the neighboring town of Foligno. There he sells the cloth and the horse and returns to Assisi with a bag of money for the priest of San Damiano so that the little church might be repaired.

When the wise priest refuses the money, fearing perhaps the wrath of Francis' father, Francis, undaunted, throws the money on the windowsill and goes up to the city of Assisi to beg for stones to personally repair the church. He heard the words; he acted on them, beginning with their literal meaning. He starts with stones for a little chapel; he ends up restoring the Catholic church itself. The literal becomes something more; the literal is the symbolic and the symbolic is the literal for Francis.

Each time he hears the word of God, he immediately responds to its literal invitation, and when he does, something much larger is fulfilled. "Blessed are the poor in spirit, for theirs is the kingdom of heaven," Jesus says (Matthew 5:3). So Francis then endeavors to be poor in spirit, but he goes further. He pushes the envelope and renounces all his possessions; he leaves the protective walls of Assisi and literally lives with the poorest of the poor outside the city wall: the lepers. Others join him in this way of life, and soon the kingdom of heaven begins to happen in the swamp-like valley below Assisi. The kingdom then begins to spread throughout Italy and Europe, the Middle East and eventually throughout the world. In Francis' response the Word of God did not return to God empty, but returned a hundredfold.

Francis follows in the footsteps of Jesus, and that is where most of us falter. We want to follow Jesus' footsteps, but we know ahead of time where they lead, and we are afraid. We hold back.

The difference between us and saints and mystics like Saint Francis is threefold: First, the mystics have heard a word beyond the word we hear in Scripture; they literally hear an inner or outer voice inviting them to love's journey. Second, the mystics fall in love with

God whom they experience in an intimate, sometimes overwhelming way. Third, they are somehow already rich soil in which the seed of God's word grows and produces rich fruit (see Matthew 13:9).

All of us are invited to be rich soil for God's word, and all of us have become rich soil in baptism. All of us have heard God's word in Scripture, in nature, in prayer, and all of us experience intimacy with God, especially in the sacraments (the external signs of a deep, interior reality). What makes the difference is both in the fullness of our response and in the level of consciousness of what is really going on within us. The kingdom of heaven is already within and around us, but because of our often lukewarm response of heart and action, we don't have eyes to see or ears to hear.

The mystics, however, cultivate awareness. They listen for God's word; they respond with concrete, often heroic, actions when they hear it. A mystic, then, is one who shows the rest of us who we really are, who we can become, if only we would realize the gift of God that is already within us and respond in our concrete daily lives to God's great gift of love. The mystic shows us how not to let God's word return to God empty. The mystic uncovers the mystery, a mystery inside each one of us, and models what it looks like and what it accomplishes.

In all of this it is important to remember that God takes the initiative—both in the ordinary believer's life and in the mystic's life. One cannot force God's hand or woo God to make one a mystic. But once that initiative is taken, the mystic's heart is changed, and he or she falls in love with God.

In Saint Francis' case God was the Poor Crucified Christ who spoke to him from the crucifix; therefore, when he would see a poor person, or one "crucified" by life's burdens or the evil of humans, he would embrace that person as he would Christ himself. The twentieth-century English mystic Caryll Houselander literally saw Christ in others from time to time, and I suspect such was Saint Francis' experience when he lived and worked mercy among the lepers.

Francis did of course have visions like the other mystics in these pages, and his first vision was when he was a young man, a knight in an Assisi regiment marching to southern Italy to fight in the papal army under Walter of Brienne. On the first night out, in the city of Spoleto near Assisi, he dreamed of a large castle hall in which there were many shields adorning the walls, which a voice assured him were for him and his followers, Francis took the voice literally and thought he was to be a great lord. But then the voice spoke again.

"What is better, Francis, to serve the lord or the servant?"

"Why, the lord, surely."

"Then why are you serving the servant? Return to Assisi and it will be shown you what you are to do."[6]

And so it was as a deserter from the army, a seeming coward or madman that Francis returned to his hometown to the ridicule of his fellow citizens.

He began to pray in caves and abandoned churches, and it was shown him what he was to do. The crucifix of San Damiano spoke to him, and sometime later, when he was riding on the road outside the city, he saw a leper by the side of the road. Inexplicably, he dismounted his horse, gave money to the leper and then embraced the leper! When he mounted his horse and turned to leave, he looked back and there was no one there. He knew then that he had embraced Christ, and he went and began to live among the lepers.

Only a madman or a man in love would do such a thing. And in a sense Francis was both; he was a man madly in love with Christ. Gradually, from the time he returned in disgrace from Spoleto, until he embraced the leper, this man who wandered the countryside of Assisi, praying in caves and abandoned chapels, had fallen in love with Christ. His life afterward was nothing but a loving response to a love that had first loved him. He wanted to be as much like his Beloved as possible, to follow in his footsteps, to listen to his words, to love as Christ had loved.

That quest for intimacy and identification with Christ is the reason for what is perceived as Francis' radicalism. He would hear a passage from the Gospel like, "whoever does not take up the cross and follow me is not worthy of me" (Matthew 10:38), and he would seek to embrace any cross that came his way in obedience to his Beloved's words. He would take literally such words as "Look at the birds of the air; they neither sow nor reap nor gather into barns, and yet your heavenly Father feeds them" (Matthew 6:26), and the birds became his brothers and sisters. He spoke to them; he blessed them; he modeled the life of his fraternity after them. And because the brothers were more important than the birds (Matthew 6:26), Francis knew the heavenly Father would care for them who, in losing their lives, would find their lives (Matthew 10:39).

Jesus himself had lived like the birds, and Francis was in love with Jesus. This is how the apostles and disciples lived, and Francis and his brothers would do the same.

In his writings Francis never uses the word *imitate* in relation to Christ; instead he uses the phrase, "to follow in the footsteps of Christ"; Christ's invitation was to "follow me" (Matthew 10:38), not "imitate me." In following Christ the self one thinks has been lost is actually found, so that one walks in the footsteps of Christ a whole and realized self.

This is the basic story of Francis of Assisi, and it is the story of the gospel lived out as fully as he was able. And in the context of that particular gospel living, there were visions and voices, culminating in Francis' mystical experience on Mount La Verna, in which he was sealed with the wounds of Christ. He returned from La Verna a stigmatic who lived intimately and excruciatingly a Christlike passion for the final two years of his life. What, then, was the mystical experience of La Verna, and what was the subsequent way of the cross he walked?

In 1224 Francis, already very ill with what was probably a form of tubercular leprosy, his eyes hemorrhaging from a trachoma contracted when he was on the Fifth Crusade, decided to make the long, almost one-hundred-mile journey from Assisi to La Verna in Tuscany—on foot!

He was discouraged by events in the order, like the building of friaries, that were to him betrayals of the gospel poverty the brothers had vowed; he was worried about the pope's call for a new crusade. What further loss of life and further divisions would result? And what would happen to his friend Sultan Malek al-Kamil, for whom Francis had promised to pray when he last left the sultan's camp?

The retreat he entered on La Verna was in preparation for the Feast of Saint Michael on September 29, and around the Feast of the

Triumph of the Holy Cross, September 14, an extraordinary mystical experience took place that is now celebrated in the Franciscan liturgical calendar on September 17.

This is Saint Bonaventure's rendering of that event:

[O]ne morning about the feast of the Exaltation of the Holy Cross, while he was praying on the mountainside, Francis saw a Seraph with six fiery wings coming down from the highest point in the heavens. The vision descended swiftly and came to rest in the air near him. Then he saw the image of a Man crucified in the midst of the wings, with his hands and feet stretched out and nailed to a cross. Two of the wings were raised above his head and two were stretched out in flight, while the remaining two shielded his body. Francis was dumbfounded at the sight and his heart was flooded with a mixture of joy and sorrow. He was overjoyed at the way Christ regarded him so graciously under the appearance of a Seraph, but the fact that he was nailed to a cross pierced his soul with a sword of compassionate sorrow.

...Eventually he realized by divine inspiration that God had shown him this vision in his providence, in order to let him see that, as Christ's lover, he would resemble Christ crucified perfectly not by physical martyrdom, but by the fervor of his spirit. As the vision disappeared, it left his heart ablaze with eagerness and impressed upon his body a miraculous likeness. There and then the marks of the nails began to appear in his hands and feet, just as he had seen them in his vision of the Man nailed to the Cross. His hands and feet appeared pierced through the center with nails, the heads of which were in the palms of his hands and on the instep of each foot, while the points stuck out on the opposite side. The heads were black and round, but the points were long and bent back, as if they had been struck with a hammer; they rose above the surrounding flesh and stood out from it. His right side seemed as if it had been pierced with a lance and was marked with a livid scar which often bled, so that his habit and trousers were stained.[7]

From this moment on, Francis realized that his desire for martyrdom had been and would continue to be fulfilled in a way other than what he expected and wanted. His martyrdom was to remain a person of peace in the face of persecution, even by his own brothers, to remain a person of peace even in war, in the crusades, in want and poverty, in sickness, in discouragement and despair. It was an inner martyrdom that leads to a transformation in Christ that is so intense and intimate that the wounds of Christ break forth from within, the outside becoming what Francis already was inside.

He was already accustomed to putting patches of soft cloth on the outside of his habit if he was wearing soft patches underneath his habit next to his skin, so that people would know that in his illness there were soft patches protecting his skin from his rough habit. Francis had always insisted on being sincere—not to be one thing on the inside and another on the outside. This, too, was a sort of martyrdom of spirit. And in the end God revealed in his flesh what Francis had already become in his spirit, a crucified son of God.

The stigmata came only at the end, two years before Francis died; it was the result of a lifetime of a living martyrdom, of remaining a person of peace, no matter what the circumstances, of sitting in peace while others were taking up arms (real or metaphorical) against their "enemies." It was the martyrdom of embracing those whom others thought repulsive; it was the martyrdom implied in the words of Jesus, "Love your enemies, do good to those who hate you" (Luke 6:27). Francis' whole life had been a living out of the gospel injunctions of Jesus so completely that he became another face of Christ for his own times and for all time.

Saint Francis never wrote of his mystical experiences, except to recount what the Lord had told him to do, where the Lord had led him. For example, in his *Testament* he writes, "For I, being in sins, thought it bitter to look at lepers, and the Lord himself led me among them, and I worked mercy with them. And when I left their company, I realized that what had seemed bitter to me, had been turned into sweetness of soul and body."[8]

But from the mystics who did write of their intimate experiences of God, we learn of the pattern and content of those mystics who did not write down their experiences. Such is the case of Saint Francis, who kept hidden the hidden things of God. It's true that others wrote about him, but Francis himself never wrote down his intimate experiences of God. In fact, he said to his brothers in his Twenty-Eighth Admonition:

Blessed are you servants who lay up treasures in heaven (cf. Mt. 6:20) of what the Lord shows you, and do not desire to show it to others hoping for personal gain from the Lord's treasure. For the same Most High will manifest your works to whomever God pleases. Blessed then are you servants who keep in your heart the secrets of the Lord. (cf. Lk. 2:19, 51; Lk. 8:15).[9]

And Saint Bonaventure, in his *Major Life of Saint Francis*, quotes Saint Francis:

When the Lord visits you in prayer, you should say, "Lord, you have sent me this comfort from heaven, even though I am a sinner and unworthy, and I entrust it to your keeping because I feel like a thief of your treasures." And when you leave your prayer, you should seem to be only a poor little sinner, and not someone especially graced by God.[10]

Both of these quotations speak to the humility of Francis, who, though he had one of the most celebrated mystical experiences of the Middle Ages in his stigmata, never spoke of it, nor wrote down what the Lord revealed to him in that intimate exchange on Mount La Verna. But a prayer attributed to Saint Francis by Saint Bernardine of Siena and Ubertino da Casale speaks volumes of what it was Saint Francis experienced on La Verna:

May the fiery and honey-sweet power of your love, O Lord, wean me from all things under heaven, so that I may die for love of your love, who deigned to die for love of my love.[11]

That, in essence, is the practical mystic, Saint Francis of Assisi.

reflection

Eyes fixed on the Lord Jesus. In this exploration of Francis the mystic, we are reminded again to look upon Christ on the cross and know that despite what things look like from a human point of view, God is love, and everything we do and everything that happens to us takes place within God's love—even to death upon a cross. Remaining in that love, no matter what befalls us, is to remain in God. The questions are not, "Why is this happening? How can God allow this? Why doesn't, didn't God prevent this?" but rather, "Can this separate me from the love of God? Is God's love still here despite this?"

God is love, and though love does not always do our will, it does not mean that God's love is not there, though that is what we feel is happening. As a man Jesus underwent this deep human experience of abandonment because the Father didn't always do what he wanted. As with us, love was not his own will. Love is the interaction between two wills; for a human being it is the interaction between my will and the One whose will is the cause of my existence and my very ability to will. Creator and creature: There is an infinite difference between them. That realization is the beginning of the love of God. And realization being of the mind, it is the beginning of truth. That something, some-one, outside myself is the cause of my very existence, makes my existence an act of gratitude for each moment held within that creative will.

The further realization that God's creative will is an eternally sustaining will, namely, that my existence will not end, summons me to humble acquiescence and dialogue—or to proud, illusory self-sufficiency, which is a kind of hell because it severs the bond of love and results in a turning in upon oneself.

God's love, in contrast to self-absorption, overflows, and though eternal creator chooses to become one with love's creation entering the created world as creative word becoming obedient to the word's own speaking of what it means to be a creature, obedient, as Saint Paul says, even "to the point of death— / even death on a cross" (Philippians 2:8). Christ was broken and died on the cross: Life did not spare the eternal Son, just as life will not spare us, but God's Incarnate Word confirmed for us that love endures, no matter what humans or fate or life does or refuses to do. And in the end obedient love rises from the grave.

chapter three

Julian of Norwich, The Goodness of God (1342–1416?)

The mystics are not those we turn to for knowledge. They are those we turn to because of their intimacy with God, because of their experience of something we all long to experience. They console with the fact that God does break into personal history. They remind us that God's Word, even in our own time, transforms hearts and souls. In the words of Jonathan Edwards, the remarkable colonial American Puritan:

> Once, as I rid out into the woods for my health, *anno* 1737; and having lit from my horse in a retired place, as my manner commonly has been, to walk for divine contemplation and prayer; I had a view, that for me was extraordinary, of the glory of the Son of God; as mediator between God and man; and his wonderful, great, full, pure and sweet grace and love, and meek and gentle condescension. This grace, that appeared to me so calm and sweet, appeared great above the heavens. The person of Christ appeared ineffably excellent, with an excellency great enough to swallow up all thought and conception. Which continued, as near

as I can judge, about an hour; which kept me, the bigger part of the time, in a flood of tears, and weeping aloud. I felt withal, an ardency of soul to be, what I know not otherwise how to express, than to be emptied and annihilated; to lie in the dust, and to be full of Christ alone; to love him with a holy and pure love; to trust in him; to live upon him; to serve and follow him, and to be totally wrapt up in the fullness of Christ; and to be perfectly sanctified and made pure, with a divine and heavenly purity. I have several other times, had views very much of the same nature, and that have had the same effects.[1]

It is this sort of experience we look for when we read the mystics, and that is why Julian of Norwich moves me so. She, like Edwards, was changed profoundly by sixteen visions she received when she was thirty-one years old. Hers is the transformation we all long for: a deeper living of life because of a heightened sense of the nearness of God. Though experienced perhaps even only once, when remembered, it affects the way we live our lives. We live true joy, no matter what trial or darkness may beset us. We experience sweetness of soul though life is bitter.

Of all the mystics treated in these pages, Julian of Norwich is perhaps the most delightful to read because of her images and the sweet charm of her narrative. She tells the story of her "Revelations of Divine Love," or "Showings," as she called them, simply but compellingly by means of homely images and metaphors whose concreteness helps us see what she saw. A further contributing factor to Julian's charm is her seemingly boundless optimism. She is by natural disposition one who sees the goodness of God everywhere. Though the love of God leads to detachment from the things of this world, they are always good things, good in themselves, created as they are by the good God, who assures her that though sin is inevitable, "all shall be well, and all shall be well, and all manner of thing shall be well."[2]

As I was beginning to sketch out a few ideas about Julian's marvelous "Showings," I was suddenly startled by the loud crow of a rooster. So out of place was this sound in the heart of Cincinnati that I wondered if I had actually heard it. But when I went to the window, there in fact were two roosters and a chicken in the yard below, one rooster crowing away, and the other rooster and the chicken pecking and scraping the ground in gleeful abandon.

The scene was so incongruous as to be medieval, and I immediately thought of the anchoress Julian hearing such a sound and going to her world-side window to peer down on the same scene. Would the sight issue for her a homely, Trinitarian image? Would it illustrate some truth God had shown her years before when she received all in a rush of five hours the first fifteen of her sixteen revelations, which she recorded in her first short manuscript of the "Showings"?

I returned to writing and intermittently checking the TV for possible white smoke from the Sistine Chapel—Pope John Paul II had died, and we were awaiting the announcement of a new pope. When I again looked out the window an hour or so later, the roosters and chicken had disappeared. Did someone come for them, or had they wandered far up the street out of sight and sound? Whatever the case, the chickens had been there, and now they were gone, and all I've written about them here is memory and interpretation and conjecture.

Julian, too, had her experiences of God's love, and recorded them in her first short manuscript, which thereby changed the experience in that she found imperfect words to describe it. Then some twenty years later—twenty years of puzzling over the meaning of her visions— she rewrote that version adding interpretation and newfound insights, thereby creating a written work twice removed from the original experience, much as the various Gospels were selective memories and interpretations and narrative transcriptions that together convey the truth and the mystery of Jesus Christ. Which brings to my mind the rooster and its inclusion in the story of Saint Peter denying Christ three times. Image builds on image, and that is the charm of Julian's "Showings," the story of her revelations imparted to her in a mystical experience.

The extraordinary effect of the "Showings" is that Julian, who lived and died in the Middle Ages, seems alive and well and talking to the reader personally today. She consoles and enlightens, she reassures, but most of all, she directs us to Christ in his passion and death; she shows how Christ's love flows in his blood poured out for us. The pain and sufferings of Christ move her to say, "[O]f all the pains that lead to salvation, this is the greatest, to see your Love suffer. How could there be greater pain than to see him suffer, who is all my life, my bliss, my joy?"[3]

Yet the revelation of Christ's suffering on the cross was an answer to Julian's own prayer to understand his passion. And when Christ grants her prayer, she is overwhelmed with her own sympathy, and she understands the compassion of Mary, the Mother of Jesus. Julian writes, "She and Christ were so one in their love that the greatness of her love caused the greatness of her suffering."[4] And like Mary, Julian keeps her eyes fixed on Jesus. "I was taught to choose Jesus for my heaven, whom I never at this time saw apart from his suffering."[5]

The content and structure of Julian's mystical life is the result of a request she made of God sometime before her revelations. She had asked for three gifts: (1) to understand Christ's passion, (2) to suffer physically while still young (she was then a woman of thirty), and (3) to have three wounds as God's gift, namely, the wound of true contrition, the wound of genuine compassion and the wound of sincere longing for God.

All three of these gifts were granted, beginning with the second, Julian's wish to suffer, and more specifically, to suffer all the pains of dying without actually dying, so that she would be cleansed to live wholly for God from that time on. That is indeed what happened, and during her sickness unto death Julian was given the revelations that are the content and shape of the "Showings."

Julian jumps right into her narrative, in medias res, in the midst of her life as a woman of thirty. "These revelations were shown to a simple and uneducated creature on the eighth of May, 1373"[6] the second version begins. There is nothing of her life up to this point because this is the beginning of what she is to relate. The mystic's real life dates from the moment God is revealed, when the world within and around the world we see with our eyes manifests its mystery. The mystery Julian sees is this: the goodness of God, who is Maker, Keeper, Lover of all that is.

It was at this time that our Lord showed me spiritually how intimately he loves us. I saw that he is everything that we know to be good and helpful. In his love he clothes us, enfolds and embraces us; that tender love completely surrounds us, never to leave us. As I saw it he is everything that is good.

And he showed me more, a little thing, the size of a hazelnut, on the palm of my hand, round like a ball. I looked at it thoughtfully and wondered, "What is this?" And the answer came, "It is all that is made." I marvelled that it continued to exist and did not suddenly disintegrate; it was so small. And again my mind supplied the answer, "It exists, both now and for ever, because God loves it." In short everything owes its existence to the love of God.

In this "little thing" I saw three truths. The first is that God made it; the second is that God loves it; and the third is that God sustains it.[7]

As so often in Julian, the number three appears here. Her truths are threefold more often than not, and her images are trinitarian.

In addition, Julian's "Showings" are intimately connected with the Passion of Christ. For example, she sees with her bodily sight Christ's bleeding head, and simultaneously God shows things to her inward sight, which she calls her ghostly sight.

All the time he was showing these things to my inward sight, I still seemed to see with my actual eyes the continual bleeding of his head. Great drops of blood rolled down from the garland like beads, seemingly from the veins; and they came down a brownish red colour—for the blood was thick—and as they spread out they became bright red, and when they reached his eyebrows they vanished. Nonetheless the bleeding continued for all the time that there were things for me to see and understand. They were as fresh and living as though they were real: their abundance like the drops of water that fall from the eaves after a heavy shower, falling so thickly that no one can possibly count them; their roundness as they spread out on his forehead were like the scales of herring. I was reminded of these three things at the time: round beads as the blood flowed, round herring scales as it spread out, and raindrops from the eaves for their abundance.[8]

Her "Showings" are this graphic and vivid, but again and again Julian insists that the things God shows her are in keeping with the teachings of the church.

I shall always believe what is held, preached, and taught by Holy Church. For the Faith of Holy Church which I had understood from the first, and which I hope by the grace of God I had consciously kept and lived by, was ever before my eyes. I was determined never to accept anything that was contrary to this, so it was with this well in mind that I looked at the revelation so diligently. And in this revelation I saw nothing counter to what had been already revealed.[9]

The whole tenor of Julian's second, longer version of the "Showings" is that of a spiritual guide who for twenty years has been meditating on her revelations, gleaning wisdom both from them and from her experience of listening to and guiding others. For example, she says that we should do three things in our own seeking: (1) By God's grace "we should seek with deliberation and diligence without slacking, and do it moreover gladly and cheerfully without moroseness or melancholy, (2) that we wait steadfastly on him in love, and do not grumble or gird against him in this life—which is not very long anyway—and (3) that we trust him wholeheartedly and confidently. This is his will."[10] Julian says further that God "works in secret, yet he wills to be seen. His appearing will be delightful and unexpected."[11]

Of the details of Julian's day-to-day life we know little; of her inner life we know much. Of her outer life we know that she was an anchoress at the Church of St. Julian in Conisford at Norwich, England. An anchoress was one who withdrew from the world into a small dwelling next to a church. It usually had a squint, or small window, that looked into the church so that she could see and hear Mass, and another window that opened to the world outside so that she could give spiritual counsel.

The ceremony for the "entombment" of an anchoress took place within the Mass and was much like a burial service. The Mass was usually the Requiem Mass, but could also be the Mass of the Holy Spirit. The anchoress candidate would make a profession; if she belonged to a religious community, she took vows; otherwise she made promises to the bishop. Then she would be clothed in a simple garb, and at the end of Mass the bishop would lead the candidate into her cell as into a tomb where she would be "dead unto the world and alive unto God."[12]

Sprinkling of holy water, incensing the candidate prostrate on the floor or on a bier, and the scattering of earth, all replicated the burial service. The bishop would then exit the cell, and the entrance would be sealed.

Such a life may seem claustrophobic to moderns, especially as we imagine that tiny cell and a lifetime's residence there. But actually the cell was not tiny, and usually it was not one room only, but several rooms with an inner courtyard or a fenced-in garden, and the anchoress often had a serving woman. Julian seemed to have had two different ones over time named Sara and Alice. Often, too, the anchoress had a cat to kill the sometimes rampant mice.

Anchoresses also had their own rule of life, the *Ancrene Riwle*, which governed the times of prayer, mainly the Divine Office, which the anchoress prayed at the appointed hours. The anchoress prayed and worked, mainly at needlework and embroidery, or taught young girls or gave spiritual instruction.

From her window Julian could look out on one of the busy roads of the city of Norwich, which in medieval times was second only to London in population. The Church of St. Julian was one of over fifty churches in Norwich and was located opposite the Augustinian friary. From her window Julian would have seen the wagons bearing corpses during the bubonic plague, which visited Norwich several times during her life. She would have seen, too, the carts of textiles, Norwich being the main English textile harbor. And from those who came to her for spiritual counsel she would have heard of the outbreak of the Hundred Years' War between France and England in 1337, and of the Great Schism, which began in 1377, with its positing of "two churches" and two popes, each regarding the other as the Antichrist.

So it was that Julian had her solitude and silence, but was not disconnected from the vibrant, troubled times in which she lived. Hers was also the time of great English writers like William Langland, John

Gower, the Gawain Poet and Geoffrey Chaucer, who was exactly her contemporary; he, the great English poet, and she the first woman to write in English. It was the time, too, of religious writers like Walter Hilton, the Wycliffe translators of the Bible, and the anonymous writer of *The Cloud of Unknowing*.

Julian's book had no title, but it came down to us as *A Book of Showings to the Anchoress Julian of Norwich*, from which we have her name (which may not even be her name but is attributed to her because her anchorage was next to the Church of St. Julian). Her book, as previously mentioned, is really two books in one, a shorter version of her sixteen revelations that she recorded shortly after their occurrence, and a longer version written some twenty years later, which is almost two and half times longer. In Julian's brief mystical experience of five hours on May 8, 1373, she received fifteen revelations, and then the final revelation the following evening. For the rest of her life she meditated on these revelations and the Lord recalled them to her mind vividly, so that in her longer version she was able to expand upon the initial revelations by commenting on them and "unpacking" them for others, presumably her spiritual counselees. (One thinks of Dante and his brief encounter with Beatrice and how his whole life and art was changed by that encounter.) One of these later meditations in Julian's longer version of the "Showings" sums up how her visions gave her the secret of prayer:

> To know the goodness of God is the highest prayer of all, and it is a prayer that accommodates itself to our most lowly needs. He does not despise the work of his hands, nor does he disdain to

serve us, however lowly our natural need may be....

For just as the body is clothed in its garments, and the flesh in its skin, and bones in their flesh, and the heart in its body, so too are we, soul and body, clothed from head to foot in the goodness of God.[13]

What is striking to me in this brief passage is Julian's holistic vision of the human person. We are not just soul; we are soul and body, and all of who we are, just as we are, is clothed in the goodness of God. There is no denigration of the body here, no puritanical squeamishness and distrust of the body because, as she points out elsewhere, Jesus was human like us, yet the fullness of the Godhead dwelled in him. And just as Jesus was one person, though human and divine in nature, so we are one person, though made of body and soul both of which are good in their making, their redeeming and their sanctifying. This is the attitude she brings to prayer; this is how she teaches us to pray: To pray is to lose oneself in the goodness of God. To do that is to be before God in gratitude and praise and to know that the good God knows who we are and what we need, and all we have to do is focus on God in all the goodness of the Trinity.

Julian's point of view reminds me of a saying of an Eastern monk that I found on a prayer card in Julian's cell at St. Julian's Church in Norwich: "Every morning put your mind into your heart and stand in the presence of God all the day long."[14] Julian would add "stand in the presence of the *good* God," even in intercessory prayer, for, intercession means simply to stand in God's presence on behalf of another. What greater or more perfect prayer could there be, then, than to put your mind in your heart and stand in the presence of the good God?

Such a stance was Julian's from the time of her "Showings" to the end of her life. As she herself said in many different ways, it is better to cling to God's goodness than to make many petitions. Julian's stance in prayer was always to simply lose herself in the goodness of God. And that is her message to us in the "Showings" she left to us. Julian summarized her basic revelation from God in these beautiful words:

> The love of God Most High for our soul is so wonderful that it surpasses all knowledge. No created being can know the greatness, the sweetness, the tenderness of the love that our Maker has for us. By his grace and help therefore let us in spirit stand and gaze, eternally marveling at the supreme, surpassing, single-minded, incalculable love that God, who is goodness, has for us. Then we can ask reverently of our lover whatever we will.[15]

reflection

What does it mean to be clothed in the goodness of God? How does Julian teach us to open ourselves to our own goodness and God's goodness within us? Over and again when we read Julian's "Showings," there is something very domestic that happens in our relationship with God. God is here in our daily lives, God is as intimate as those in our closest relationships, as our pets are, like the cats that lived in Julian's cell. Everything and everyone reminds us of God's intimate care, even the smallest thing, as she reminds us, though it be as small as the merest hazelnut. When we have eyes to see, and we see in love, the whole world speaks of God, a God who clothes everything in goodness. And all this goodness leads us back to God. As Julian says so beautifully,

> I saw that he is at work unceasingly in every conceivable thing, and that it is all done so well, so wisely, and so powerfully that it is far greater than anything we can imagine, guess, or think. Then we can do no more than gaze in delight with a tremendous desire to be wholly united to him, to live where he lives, to enjoy his love, and to delight in his goodness. It is then that we, through our humble, persevering prayer, and the help of his grace, come to him now, in this present life. There will be many secret touches that we shall feel and see, sweet and spiritual, and adapted to our ability to receive them. This is achieved by the grace of the Holy Spirit, both now and until the time that, still longing and loving, we die. On that day we shall come to our Lord knowing our self clearly, possessing God completely. Eternally "hid in God" we shall see him truly and feel him fully, hear him spiritually, smell him delightfully, and taste him sweetly! We shall see God face to face, simply and fully.[16]

chapter four

JACOPONE DA TODI, THE MADNESS OF GOD (1230?–1306)

If there is an epithet for the poetry of the medieval Franciscan Jacopone da Todi, it is surely, "Poet of the Madness of Love."[1] The mad lover is God, whose love is so great that in Jesus Christ God embraces the cross as *the* place where God and humans meet. It is God who descends to us, not we who ascend to God. Because the cross is the place par excellence of this descent, God's overflowing love is proven there more than anywhere else.

In Jacopone's poems love is God's motivation. Like a lover drunk with love, God begs the love of the human being. God woos humankind, begs us to love him. Why, then, do we refuse his love, betray him, show contempt for his love? God is in pain because we don't return such infinite love. God speaks:

"Is there any greater sign
That Love could have given
Than to become the last,
The most derelict of men?

"Who would ever be mad enough
To turn himself into an ant
So as to save an army of ants,
An undeserving, ungrateful army of ants?

"My madness was greater yet:
To abase Myself
To take this road
and become a suffering man.

"I did not love you for My pleasure,
I loved you for yourself;
What I did for you
added nothing to My joy."

. . .

"Love drew Me to you,
That you might be remade...."

. . .

"This love lays down no conditions,
demands no interest;
It is total union,
and knows not change.[2]

Jacopone's poetry is heavily narrative. He tells the story, often through dialogues like the ones between the lover and the beloved, a story of God's complete engagement with and marriage to humankind. Sin is to betray this incredible love that is given to us in Jesus Christ. When we realize our betrayal, self-hatred is our natural response: How could we have been indifferent to such a love? We are not so much aware of transgressing a moral law as rejecting a relationship.

The extremes of self-hatred in much medieval mysticism is not hatred of self or of the body for being bad in itself. It is hatred of my heart that could have been so blinded by the unruly desires of the body as to not see how good I am, how beautiful, that even God has fallen in love with me, and I turned elsewhere for love. Jacopone writes:

> Weep, suffer and sigh,
> For you have lost your gentle Lord;
> May these tears yet bring Him back
> To my disconsolate heart.
> ...
> For I have lost both son and father.
> Comely Christ, lily in flower,
> has left me, and the fault is mine.[3]

And blessed Christ answers,

> Though you cast Me out with malice,
> Because of your repentance I shall return,
> So that someone like you can never complain
> that I betrayed a loyal love.[4]

Again and again in his love dialogues between God and us, Jacopone sings of God's madness—love that never ceases no matter what. It is eternal and is not dependent on our acceptance. When we repent of our refusals of the lover, it is not as though now God's love returns. It has always been there and always will be, but we perceive Christ as returning. What changes is us. We let that love love us, transform us, and the place of that transformation is the cross because that is the place of God's greatest love.

We all know the expression, "Love me, love my dog." In the same way it is as if Christ were saying, "Love me, love my cross." Our love of the cross does not derive, therefore, from our hatred of ourselves, but from our love of him who loved us here, in this place, this reality we call the cross.

Jacopone praises the human person as one who is made by God and is made to see God. With him the medieval *Lauda* (a song of praise) becomes not just a song of praise of God, but also a song about the praise God gives us by willing to be united with us in love. God is totally devoted to us. God gives love upon love in order to receive our love. In an extraordinary inversion, God becomes the "victim" of the love of the bride. Jesus says,

> If I become man, man will attain to his proper end;
> The act of submission to God will be Mine.[5]

In the Incarnation we finally meet our heart's longing: God. And Christ, who is God, because he is also human, will submit to God. In Christ, we submit to God who has first submitted to our humanity. In Christ both God and humankind are satisfied. Each reaches the pinnacle of Love. Jacopone has Christ say,

> I've let it be known that all men must come
> To learn from Me the things of God;
>
> ...
>
> I come to teach men how to love;
> He who masters this art abides with God—
> If he holds fast, he will know eternal joy.[6]

In Christ God becomes the mad, reckless lover:

> My bride, the wonder of this exchange of love!
>
> When you beseech Me, you command Me;
>
> Love makes Me suffer, drives Me mad,
>
> Drawing Me outside of Myself and closer to you.[7]

It is this kind of love that explains Jacopone's own madness, the trajectory of his life, the extremes of his passions, his cry to Christ:

> Show me where my Lord is, I have heard He loves me;
>
> Tell me where to find Him, I can wait no more.
>
> Long it is He waits for Me in sorrow.

And Christ answers:

> Soul, since you have come to Me,
>
> Gladly will I answer you. Come,
>
> See, this is My bed—the cross.
>
> Here we will be one, Come to Me
>
> And I will quench your thirst.[8]

In the poems of Jacopone, it is almost as if humankind is God's god. God does not even spare his own Son to gain our love. Such love so overwhelms Jacopone that he cries out to Christ,

> Were these the actions of someone drunk, or out of his senses?
>
> How could You abdicate kingdom and riches,
>
> A renunciation that verges on madness?[9]

Christ answers,

> For love of you, for your sake,
>
> I accept need, shame, and servitude.
>
> …
>
> Give Me love, I beseech you, My Bride,
>
> It is love I desire; I ask for no more.
>
> Love has no mercy—it strips Me,
>
> Binds Me, enflames Me ceaselessly.
>
> Love Me then, My much-loved bride:
>
> I bought you dearly, and have given you all.[10]

And this is Jacopone's response:

> O my love, naked will I scale that cross,
>
> To suffer and die with You.
>
> Lord, clasped close in Your embrace,
>
> In joy will I suffer and die.[11]

So it was with Jacopone, whose life was an icon of one who scaled the cross with Christ, his beloved lover.

What, then, was the outer life of Blessed Jacopone da Todi, whose inner life we have been looking at so closely? He was born Jacopo dei Benedetti sometime in the 1230s in the Italian hill town of Todi in Umbria. Son of wealthy parents, he lived a life of leisure and luxury and from his youth was drawn to the works of the Sicilian poets who produced the first significant body of Italian poetry. Influenced by the troubadours of Provence, they were called Sicilian, not necessarily as a geographical designation, but because they were under the patronage of the Emperor Frederick II, who, though his official court was in

Sicily, moved constantly from one part of the vast Holy Roman Empire to another. As this portable Sicilian court moved through Italy, Frederick's entourage made a profound impression on northern and central Italy, including the countryside of Todi in Umbria.

There is no doubt that the young Jacopo learned from the Sicilian school much of what he knew of poetry, especially the language of love in which women were the objects of the poet's passion, and the poet's own subjective state was the center of the poem. Later when Jacopone wrote his own love poems, he replaced women with God, drawing upon the experience and style of the Sicilian poets, many of whose themes were reflected in his work. Medieval historian and Jacopone da Todi biographer, George T. Peck, enumerates these themes as:

1. Love is fire that burns.
2. The heart of a lover is like a furnace.
3. The fire of love melts the heart of the poet as wax or a candle is burnt.
4. Love is full of paradoxes. It is like peace and yet like a battle; it is wounded, but wounds.
5. The service of love is like service to a feudal lord.
6. Love is full of joy, but love is also full of sorrow, the sorrow of separation and loss.[12]

Furthermore, the dramatic dialogue, the *tenson*, which was a frequently used form in both Sicilian and Provençal poetry, was one of Jacopone's favorite means of expression.

However, poetry was but an avocation for Jacopo. He was by profession a brilliant lawyer and notary much sought after in Todi. Around

1267 he married Vanna di Guidone, a beautiful woman with a beautiful soul who was killed when the balcony beneath her collapsed at a party she was attending. When the devastated Jacopo carried her home and was preparing her for burial, he found a hair shirt (made of rough animal hair worn against the skin for mortification and penance) beneath her costly dress, and his whole world collapsed. He realized the folly of his life up to that point. He renounced his former way of life, donned the habit of a Franciscan tertiary, and began to wander about like a madman, begging and wearing tattered clothes. The children of Todi dubbed him "Jacopone" ("Stupid Jacopo"), and the name stuck.

After ten years as a mad beggar and secular Franciscan, Jacopone asked to be admitted as a simple lay brother in the Franciscan convent of San Fortunato at Todi. Despite his eccentricities, he was accepted and embraced the chaste life of extreme poverty and obedience. As his balance began to return, Jacopone started to write *Laude*, popular, psalm-like poems. Of the some two hundred *Laude*, those set to music were among the best-loved hymns of Umbria.

Unlike the refined Sicilian poets, Jacopone used the rough and expressive words of his native Umbrian dialect. In the spirit of his founder, Saint Francis, he wanted to get his message across to the poor and the rich, the uneducated and the educated. He was attuned to the popular culture that sprang up in Todi after the collapse of the court of Frederick II (sometime after 1250) when jugglers, minstrels, acrobats, storytellers and fools took to the roads to entertain in the piazzas of Italian towns like Todi. He wanted to be like the singers of popular tales who had become fixtures of the town scene.

Jacopone took the wordy, repetitious, popular *Lauda* and made it into an art form. Unlike the popular *Laude* he heard in the piazzas of Todi, Jacopone's are extremely personal, complicated in their thought, compressed, subtle in their interiority. In the words of Angelo of Monteverdi, "He kept the popular tone, and accepted its simple and coarse form; but he knew how to pour into it, with a robust art, the full-ness of his soul—drunk with divine love, pervaded by the hatred . . . of human miseries and vanity, conscious of the value of his loves and hates, and expertly learned in the secrets of the mystic life."[13]

Meanwhile, during his years as a Franciscan, Jacopone was drawn to the so-called Spiritual Franciscans, a group of friars who rejected a more moderate living of the Rule of Saint Francis and tried to recreate the spirit and the letter of Saint Francis and his first companions. Some of the Spiritual Franciscans ran afoul of the other friars. A group of them appealed to Pope Celestine, a saintly man, to favor their inter-pretation of the Rule of Saint Francis. The pope went further; he allowed them to start their own community called the Celestines. But Celestine, an ascetic contemplative at heart, soon resigned the papacy and paved the way for the ascendancy of Pope Urban VIII, an acquisi-tive, greedy man who immediately rescinded the acts of Pope Celestine, including the community of Celestines, ordering them back to the Franciscans. Some fled into exile and others were reconciled with the Order of Saint Francis.

Jacopone, in the meantime, entered the fray and began to write satires and polemic poems against Urban, attacking the legitimacy of his election and even accusing him of heresy. He joined forces with the Colonna family who were attempting to bring down the avaricious Urban, even calling for a council in which the cardinals could revote.

In the end, Urban crushed militarily the Colonna uprising, and Jacopone was imprisoned in one of the friaries, deprived of the sacraments and kept in solitary confinement for five years.

During the years of his imprisonment, Jacopone appealed twice to the pope for pardon, but Urban refused. In the end Urban himself was brought down by plotters, led by Sciarra Colonna, a French ruffian named Guglielmo di Nogaret and the papal captain of Ferentino. They seized Anagni, home to a popular papal palace, on September 7, 1303, and cornered the pope in his own palace. He was flanked by the only two cardinals still loyal to him, and was dragged off to Rome under the charge of the Orsini cardinals. He refused to eat for fear of poison and took to his room where he died on the thirty-fifth day of his imprisonment. By then he was out of his mind, believing that anyone who came near him was going to take him to prison.

A gentle man, Cardinal Niccolo Boccasini, was elected pope to succeed Urban, taking the name Benedict XI. It was he who finally freed Jacopone, who retired to the hill village of Collazzone, about eight miles up the Tiber Valley from Todi. He lived there the last three years of his life in the company of several friars attached to the convent of San Lorenzo di Collazzone.

Over a hundred years after his death in 1306 (he was already revered by some as a saint), Jacopone's remains were found in the convent of Santa Maria di Montecristo, where the sisters of San Lorenzo had taken them when their own convent began to decline. In 1596 the tomb where his remains had been reburied (in the crypt of the Franciscan church of San Fortunato in Todi) was finally dedicated with fitting ecclesiastical ceremonies.

Today Jacopone da Todi is known, for the most part, only for his great poem "Stabat Mater Dolorosa," which countless faithful world-wide have sung during Holy Week. It is a poem of compassion for the sorrowful mother of Jesus, standing beneath his cross. Franciscans recognize him as among the blessed of the Franciscan Order, though he's never been formally beatified by the church, and as one of the greatest poets of the Order, whose *Laude* continue to be sung and loved, especially in Italy. One of these could stand as Jacopone's own epitaph:

> O Love, divine Love, why do You lay siege to me?
> In a frenzy of love for me, You find no rest.
>
> From five sides You move against me,
> Hearing, sight, taste, touch, and scent.
> To come out is to be caught; I cannot hide from You.
>
> If I come out through sight, I see Love
> Painted in every form and color,
> Inviting me to come to You, to dwell in You.
>
> If I leave through the door of hearing,
> What I hear points only to You, Lord;
> I cannot escape love through this gate.
>
> If I come out through taste, every flavor proclaims:
> "Love, divine Love, hungering Love!
> You have caught me on Your hook, for You want to reign in me."
>
> If I leave through the door of scent,
> I sense you in all creation; You have caught me
> And wounded me through that fragrance.

If I come out through the sense of touch
I find Your lineaments in every creature;
To try to flee from You is madness.

Love, I flee from You, afraid to give You my heart:
I see that You make me one with You;
I cease to be and can no longer find myself.

If I see evil in a man or defect or temptation,
You fuse me with him, and make me suffer;
O Love without limits, who is it You love?

It is You, O Crucified Christ,
Who take possession of me,
Drawing me out of the sea to the shore;

There I suffer to see Your wounded heart.
Why did you endure the pain?
So that I might be healed.[14]

reflection

In Jacopone da Todi we see graphically that the mystic and those who are close to God always feel utterly unworthy and small compared to their tremendous Lover. But that unworthiness is not because they are not good or that they don't amount to anything, but rather their unworthiness derives from the beauty and worthiness of the Lover. The mystics are unanimous in the almost extreme sense of their own sinfulness once God has revealed something of the Divine presence to them. So good and beautiful and full of overflowing love is God that one feels unclean, imperfect, even ugly and foul, and one begins to see and remember one's sins.

The awareness of God is like the awareness that you are falling in love with a beautiful person whose worthiness, goodness and beauty are so overwhelming that you wonder how so extraordinary a person could possibly love you, whose whole life up to this moment has been lived unworthily of such a love. And when that person is God, and you're aware that God created you, died for you, and through the Holy Spirit is drawing you into deeper intimacy, you are flooded with regret for the infidelity of really not believing for so long what you now know: God is love, is, in fact, in love with you and wants your love in return.

So it is not self-hatred that leads you to God. It is the realization of God's love that suddenly forces you to see your own wretchedness apart from so great a love. Nor is this grief and regret a permanent state, for God soon shows you that you have been forgiven even before you were aware of your infidelity. You were lovable to God before you began to see your own worth, which God soon reveals to you. You pass from hatred of your own sins to love of the divine lover who, in revealing his countenance to you, has shown you what real love is and how far you are from that kind of love.

You move from self-absorption to absorption in the lover. That love now preoccupies your thoughts while at the beginning you were aware only of your own unworthiness, of the infinite gap between what you thought love was, or life was, and what it really is.

God does not want you to live miserably aware of your sins but only to know the love that moves all things, as Dante says. You grieve, you feel sorrow, you begin to change. And the change is, above all, a focusing on God rather than on yourself, and on returning the love with which you are loved.

At first you are wholly aware of God's presence, but that, too, is prelude. For soon what you knew and felt you have to take on faith. For God will remove his face from you, the face that gave you so much consolation, so that you will begin to love God for God's sake and not for the consolation and peace and sense of importance that derives from being specially loved.

Always it is God who leads, God who takes the initiative, and no amount of penance or prayer can twist God's arm, as it were, and take control into your own hands. You may wrestle with God, but you are wounded in the process and still God is seemingly no longer for you as God was when you suddenly knew God's love for you.

Like any love relationship, the honeymoon does not last. It is the love in good times and bad that lasts—or doesn't—if it was all about you and your pleasure and comfort from the beginning.

The contours of the journey of love are pretty much the same; the particulars depend on the personality and character of the one who falls in love with God. The image that works best for me—and there are many images—is that of a small boat at sea, which is me, traversing calm to stormy seas, with every weather in between. The constant is not God's power, but God's love, no matter how well or poorly I navigate those seas.

It's easy to believe God's love and to feel God's presence when the seas are calm and the sun is out, and I'm relaxed and feeling safe and warm and flooded with light. It's harder when the storms begin. The larger and better built the ship, the more easily and surely do I cross rough seas. The large ship is well built with virtues that expand the self and deepen its hull. Such a metaphor is a cliché, but cliché or not, it corresponds to the way I experience the journey with God and in God.

You may have another way of articulating your life's journey—a way much more technologically advanced—but the personal experience and knowledge is the same: Of faith, hope and love, the greatest is love (see 1 Corinthians 13:13).

Love keeps you busy tending to the ship rather than worrying about yourself—whether, for example, you have enough faith and hope. Love also builds up all the other virtues, including faith and hope. Love keeps you aware of the weather but not preoccupied with it.

Then, no matter what the weather, there is love, for Divine love sustains God's creatures in every weather. Once we realize this fundamental truth, then the world is transformed, and we praise God in and through and with all creatures.

As Jacopone writes,

I sense You in all creation; You have caught me
And wounded me through that fragrance.

...

I find your lineaments in every creature.

...

It is You, O Crucified Christ,
Who take possession of me,
Drawing me out of the sea to the shore.[15]

chapter five

CATHERINE OF SIENA, THE HIDDEN THINGS OF GOD[1] (1347–1380)

When I was a young boy living in Gallup, New Mexico, in the 1940s, I had no inkling of the spiritual awakening that would illumine my young life. From a boy who loved to play "cowboys and Indians" and fish and hunt with my dad, who loved to act out skits on neighbors' porches and hang out after school with the military police at the Santa Fe Railroad depot, I suddenly became aware of the immediate and close presence of Jesus and Mary, of the saints whose pictures I would subsequently hang on the walls of my room like sports heroes or movie stars, of the call of God to become a priest in the footsteps of Saint Francis and of the Franciscans stationed at St. Francis of Assisi Church.

This vivid sense of God's presence and of the protection and guid-ance of the saints precipitated a need to know more about who God is, who the saints are, so I began to read spiritual books voraciously, the lives of the saints especially. If they wrote their own lives, like Saint

Thérèse of Lisieux, I read and reread their words, but always with a tinge of fear that I might have to suffer what they suffered. But only a *tinge* of fear, and that was soon displaced by the conviction that God would give me the grace, as God gave me this feeling—and it was a feeling—that God would always be there tangibly.

This childhood experience led me at age fourteen to leave home and travel fifteen hundred miles on a Greyhound bus to the Franciscan seminary in Cincinnati, Ohio, to begin a thirteen-year pilgrimage to ordination as a Franciscan priest, a pilgrimage that would be anything but what I had anticipated when I boarded the bus, all pumped up to become a saint and bring God to the world. How bitter and sweet would be the lesson that it is God's will that brings us peace and joy and not our own grandiose, adolescent will for fame or spiritual power or holiness.

At this remove it is difficult to reconstruct those years when I was entering adolescence and experiencing all the confusion and sexual awakening of any boy and at the same time being taught and encouraged in the way of chastity that one day I would have to vow as a way of life. My only defense, and this was largely my own doing, against the strong sexual urge was a subtle "denial" of my own body and an almost violent will to separate my body from the spiritual world I was trying to live in. I prayed and fasted, practiced custody of the eyes, as it was then called, and confessed every thought that might have had even a tinge of sex in it. Because I was an adolescent, sex was *the* sin, and also because I was an adolescent, I was obsessed with ridding myself of sexual thoughts and actions.

What I did not understand then was that asceticism is not an endeavor to punish the evil body, but an attempt to shatter the illusion that we are simply our bodies. Asceticism strives to break the body's hold on us so that the spiritual can break through. The body's dominion prevents the spirit from revealing its presence in and through the body, or, more accurately, that we are not just body, but body and soul, the two not split, but one person, integrated only when body and soul have their say in a healthy, love-filled way.

The integration of soul and body that ensued during the thirteen years I prepared for ordination to the priesthood was a journey not unlike the journey that mystics describe. Their extreme penances and some of their attitudes toward the world and the body sometimes remind me of my own misdirected penances as a boy and make me suspicious at times of their motivation. I try in these pages to discern between healthy and unhealthy penance, as I had to do in my own life and journey toward a holistic spirituality.

With Saint Catherine of Siena we enter the world of the body: the world of birthing and nourishing, the world of the beloved and the lover, of the betrothal and mystical marriage. At the time of Catherine the body was seen variously as a residence as complex as a palace or church with a hierarchy of spaces within, as a temple within which one conversed with Christ in Holy Communion, as the skin that enclosed the soul as strictly as the walls of a fortress or a monastic cloister.

Of all these images the one most frequently used by Catherine was the body as the cloistered cell within which she conversed intimately with Christ, who had appeared to her when, as a child of six, she was walking home with her younger brother. From that moment on, until she was twenty years old, her life was an ever-increasing move inward to the place of her encounters and ongoing relationship with the Christ of her visions. And what a visionary she was!

But in her twentieth year, Christ, who by then had become her bridegroom in a profound mystical marriage, told her she was from then on to move beyond the cloister of her soul into the world at large and minister to others as he had during the years of his public ministry. This Catherine did with a zeal that embraced first the members of her family, then the citizens of Siena, the warring factions of Siena and Florence, and ultimately, the church itself in her efforts to bring the pope back from the so-called Avignon Captivity, which had begun when Urban V left Rome for France in 1309, and she saw happen in the person of Gregory XI, who finally returned the papacy to Rome from Avignon, France, a few years before Catherine's death in Rome at the age of thirty-three.

The details of this inner and outer life are most interesting and illuminating for us living seven hundred years after the fourteenth century, which the historian Barbara Tuchman called a "distant mirror"[1] of the twentieth century. Catherine's life, in fact, reads like the life of a heroine in a fairy tale. So, like a teller of fairy tales, I begin this story at the very beginning.

Catherine Benincasa was born the twenty-fourth child of a family of twenty-five children, a prosperous wool-dyer's family of the Italian city of Siena. Her three-story family home still stands, an emblem of the prominence of the Benincasa family, whose name means "well-housed."

Her first years were those of a lively, much-loved child who delighted in her family. Then one day, when she was six years old,

Catherine and her younger brother were walking home; suddenly she saw in a vision Christ wearing a papal tiara. From that moment on Catherine began to change. When she was seven, she made a vow of perpetual virginity, and when she entered adolescence, her mother had to cajole her into washing properly and caring for her hair.

I remember, as a young seminarian, thinking that this was not the saint to emulate. She seemed wildly crazy to me, a young girl not unlike a deranged young woman in a horror movie, or like the mad woman in the attic of Charlotte Brontë's *Jane Eyre*. I was not alone in my judgment.

Catherine seemed so indifferent to men that her mother, alarmed, as I was in reading about her, decided to elicit the help of Catherine's married sister, of whom the young Catherine was very fond. Her sister instructed her in the ways of a young woman, and for a while Catherine made half-hearted efforts to conduct herself like her contemporaries of marriageable age. But when her sister died unexpectedly in childbirth, the household was turned upside-down, and the family decided it was time for Catherine to marry. She, however, rebelled and, with the encouragement of her confessor, cut off her hair.

Outraged, her parents relegated her to the job of a servant in the home and, much like Cinderella, she was subjected to ridicule and taunts. But Catherine entered wholeheartedly into her new role, thinking of her family as the holy family of Nazareth whom she was appointed to serve. She was also at this time deprived of her own room, which she countered by imagining an inner room, a cell located in a private place inside her heart where she prayed and communed with

God. How often, in our own times, do women and men alike yearn for a room of their own, away from the noise and busyness of life, and find it only within, in the room of prayer and contemplation.

Catherine's goal at this time was to join the lay Dominicans, a group of local women who served the poor while living a consecrated life at home. But because of her youth and beauty, the Dominicans were reluctant to accept her, until Catherine was struck with a disease, probably chicken pox, which left her face disfigured.

Her family, too, eventually approved of Catherine's entrance into the Dominican Third Order, and after her father had seen a dove hovering over her as she prayed, she was again allowed to have her own room. Almost immediately her inner life began to blossom, and she experienced so many and such vivid visions that she began to doubt that they were of God. But Jesus reassured her that they were real because of her humility, and he gave her a rule of thumb for discerning the authenticity of her visions: She was to remember that she is one who is not, and God is the one who is. If she held on to that knowledge, the enemy would never deceive her.

Some cringe when they hear, "You are she who is not," because they hear these words psychologically. They hear, "You're nothing; you don't matter." But those living in the medieval era did not hear these words psychologically, nor was that the intention of God in uttering them to Catherine. The words are metaphysical; they refer to the infinite distance between the Creator and the creature, between the one who is ("I AM I WHO AM," God says to Moses in Exodus 3:14) and the one who is not, as compared to the one who is. We are completely dependent for our existence, for our ability to say, "I am," upon the one who is pure being, who alone can say, "I AM."

Medieval mystics, and in particular Catherine, had a strong sense of self. They were not "ones who were not" in their relationships with others, only in their relationship to God. Catherine was a strong, formidable woman who knew who she was as a woman among men and women, but she also knew who she was as a creature of God. She was of God, but not God.

If she was tempted to think that her visions made her someone special or better than others, she very soon learned that visions are not all sweetness and light. At one point in the three years of solitude in her cell, the sweet presence of Christ was replaced with demonic visions and voices, including vivid visions of naked couples copulating all around her cell. The buzzing in her ears, too, became so bad that she left her room and sought out churches where she could remain and pray without demonic oppression. But as soon as she returned home to her room, the demons would start assaulting and tempting her again.

No doubling of her prayers and petitions helped. In the end, when she was about to succumb to complete exhaustion, she remembered to remember that she was the one who was not, and she threw herself upon the mercy of God, trusting wholly in her beloved. She then told the demons to do with her as they pleased; she found them merely amusing! Almost immediately the demonic visions and voices began to diminish and disappear.

Later in her life Catherine said that what was terrifying in this experience was not the presence of demons but that they were in her mind, and she did not yet know that she was not her mind. She was able to mock them at last because she could distance herself from her own thoughts. Thoughts change, but the center of who we are, the self, transcends and is more permanent than changeable, fleeting thoughts.

We all have experiences analogous to Catherine's. For example, there is something we've been afraid of all our lives, something that terrifies us, and we keep running from it, letting it tyrannize our minds. Then one day we turn around and face what has been pursuing us, and there's no one there, or what is there is much smaller, much less threatening than what our minds have made of it. God told Catherine not to argue or get into a conversation with the demons because they would then have a hold on her. But throwing herself upon the one who *is*, and then mocking the demons who are powerless without God, the demons themselves were rendered powerless over her.

Of course, some readers, I'm sure, see in Catherine every sign of psychosis: the split personality, hearing voices, demonic visions and a mystical marriage. The signs, to be sure, are there, but even if her experiences up to this point had proven to be temporary mental illness (which they were not), what happens next locates Catherine among the saints and intimates of God.

In a series of visions and intimate conversations with Christ, Catherine is betrothed to Jesus, who then weds her in a profound mystical marriage, giving her a ring made of the circumcised foreskin of the infant Jesus. Catherine literally put on the flesh of Christ, becoming his bride. On another occasion when Catherine had prayed for a clean heart, Christ took her heart for a few days then brought it back. It beat, she said, louder and more strongly than before, and she knew she had been given the heart of Christ to love others. Both of these visions may still seem madness to some, psychological projections of a twisted young mind. But the most convincing proof that Catherine had not "gone around the bend," irretrievably lost in some self-absorbed inner world, occurred when she was in her twentieth year. Christ appeared at the threshold of her cell, but did not enter. He asked her to come out of her cell, and from then on she was to love him by loving others. She was to live, as he had, a public life of service, which Catherine did selflessly and heroically, dying in Rome thirteen years later, like Jesus, in her thirty-third year.

Teresa of Avila says that in true prayer one enters in, remains a while, and then has the good sense to know when to come out. Jesus is Catherine's good sense, as he is ours. The pattern of his own life of prayer is what he now offers to Catherine: going aside to pray but then returning to the highways and byways of the world to preach and heal and minister to others, then going aside again, then coming out to minister—over and over again the same pattern of prayer and charity, charity and prayer, neither one wholly separated from the other. For when we pray, we are exercising charity, and when we act charitably, we are praying—though there are times when prayer predominates and times when action predominates. Neither one is possible for any length of time without the other.

What Catherine experienced in her years of solitude in her cell was an uncovering, through visions, of what is going on in all of us but what we don't have eyes to see: the battle between God and Satan, the intimacy with God that we experience most tangibly in the Eucharist, the transformation into Christ that takes place imperceptibly and is only revealed by the fruits of our lives, our virtues and goodness, the love we show to others in concrete acts.

All of us, in one sense, are like Catherine of Siena. Some of us succumb to Satan in the end; most of us come out the other end of temptation, sin and forgiveness as persons less self-absorbed, more giving,
more loving, more aware of our union with Christ in his everyday life,
his passion and death, and in his resurrected life. We come to know
who we are by learning that we are not, except in God who *is.*

And most of us are not as heroic as Catherine was in the active life
of service Christ invited her to. Catherine, reminiscent of her first
vision at age six when she saw Christ wearing the papal tiara, was to be
instrumental in bringing the pope back to Rome from Avignon, end-
ing the Avignon Captivity.

In the meantime she threw herself into reconciling family feuds,
city feuds, feuds and wars between cities, bringing healing, both physical and spiritual, to countless people. But her greatest challenge was
surely to bring peace and reconciliation within Christendom. She
worked for the return of the papacy to Rome, the establishment of
peace among warring factions in Italy and Europe, and fostered a crusade to bring Christianity to Muslims. This latter was not a military
crusade, but an outreach, an evangelization of Muslims and their sultan with words and example, much as Francis had done.

On April 1, 1375, Catherine, like Saint Francis, had a vision in
which she received the sacred stigmata and prophesied the Great
Schism (the existence of two popes), which came to pass four years
later. In 1378 Catherine finally succeeded in persuading the Avignon
pope, Gregory XI, to return to Rome. Gregory died almost immediately
thereafter, in March of that year; his successor, Urban VI, proved so
incompetent that the cardinals elected a new pope in September, and

the Great Schism began. Catherine remained loyal to Urban as the true pope and came to Rome at his request to live out her final years. She spent those years offering her life in expiation for the sins of the church, a heavy burden on her heart to the very end. Shortly before she died, Catherine was looking at a mosaic in St. Peter's Basilica of the apostles buffeted in a storm at sea. Suddenly their little bark, the church, detached itself from the mosaic and rested on her shoulders. She felt the full weight of it and fell to the floor paralyzed with pain. Taken back to her cell, she lingered for weeks, then died on April 29, 1380.

Two things stand out graphically in Catherine's life: the intensity of her penances, which are off-putting to most people today, and the almost incredible vividness and plethora of details of her visions which would drive most people irreversibly inward toward madness or toward living in a world akin to the imaginary, fairy-tale world of a child. But Catherine's visions are the private world from which she emerges to engage the world outside with the energy and skill of a modern, globe-trotting diplomat, politician or troubleshooter. Like Thomas More, she could surely have been chancellor of England (even under Henry VIII!), or any other country and still, like him, have maintained a rich inner life.

Her outer life is an open book, so to speak, but what about the life in that other book, her *Dialogue*, the dictated record of her ecstatic inner life? Of the mystics we consider here, Catherine is one of the most prolific in recording her mystical experiences. The *Dialogue*, though its images are often homey and original, is both long and complex and can only be read in small doses. At least that is my experience.

Catherine had begun composing her *Dialogue* before she came to Rome in 1378, at a castle outside Siena, where she had made peace between warring factions of her own family. She calls the manuscript simply "the book," or "my book." It was her confessor and first biographer, Raymond of Capua, who gave it the title *Dialogue*. It consists of conversations between the eternal Father and Catherine, whom he calls "His very dear daughter, and His much loved child." Copied down by others when Catherine spoke in ecstasy, the book's motif is the mercy of God, summed up in these words of the Father: "I have told you that I will show the world mercy so that you can see that mercy is the sign by which I am known."[2]

The symbol that centers God's mercy is the bridge, which is Christ, God's Son. Catherine develops this symbol in several ways that have been brilliantly summarized by Sigrid Undset in her biography of Saint Catherine (the only book on Saint Catherine that was not off-putting to me as a young seminarian). Undset expounds on the image of the bridge and shows its richness as a symbol of our intimacy with God. The steps of the bridge are sometimes seen as ascending the bridge of the cross, kissing first Christ's feet, then the wound in his side, then his mouth. These three steps stand for stages toward union with God: The first is fear of God's punishment, which has already led us to the foot of the cross; the second symbolizes faithful but imperfect service in following Christ that is still motivated in part by the hope of the reward we will receive; and the third step is the love of God for who God is and not for God's gifts.

Elsewhere in *Dialogue* the three steps are symbols for qualities of the soul—memory, intelligence and will—which Catherine says, extrapolating on a passage from Scripture, bring union with Christ, "For when two or three are gathered in my name, I am there among them" (Matthew 18:20), the two or three being memory, intelligence and will. One can see how effectively these three worked in Catherine's visions: (1) the memory of the vision, (2) the intelligence to discern what was of God and what was of Satan, and (3) the will to follow through on the vision's message and implications.

The original *Dialogue* is written in Catherine's beautiful Tuscan dialect, which, like any language well-spoken, is impossible to translate adequately. The book is one of the masterpieces of Italian literature.

What to make, then, of this great mystic and her revelations? The lifestyle of the mystics, whether medieval or modern, is often shocking or at least pushes the envelope of credibility. When one looks at the events of Catherine's life, beginning already with her vision at the age of six, one is tempted to say that they derive mainly from the imagination of her first biographer who wrote with the uncritical piety of medieval hagiographers whose proclivity to interpret unusual happenings in terms of the supernatural is akin to moderns' tendency to reduce the extraordinary to the psychological or to seek a scientific explanation for everything.

Catherine's actions are, from the modern point of view, extreme. Yet we see the same kind of extremes in the lives of modern mystics like Simone Weil and Caryll Houselander, both of whom were anything but uncritical in their assessment of their lives and both of whom lived under the critical psychological and scientific scrutiny of others. But the test of their authenticity is the same as it is for all of us: charity. The visions and ecstasies of the true mystics do not debilitate charity, do

not make them less able to holistically respond to Christ's two commandments to love God with our whole heart and mind and soul and to
love our neighbor as ourselves.

On the contrary, the mystics' visionary life makes them more
charitable, more energized for others. For one thing, their ecstasies
are usually comparatively brief—they do not live in perpetual ecstasy.
Second, though the mystic may seem wholly debilitated, almost com-
atose during the ecstasy, the true mystic afterward returns to an
intense gospel life of service to others, especially the sick and those
on the margins of society, or to involvement with the social and eccle-
sial problems of his or her time. The ecstasy or vision, in other words,
does not drive the mystic inward to self-centeredness, but takes her
out of herself into God, only to return recharged, as it were, with
increased love of God's creatures. The true vision is God's work,
God's initiative, not the result of a diseased mind. It leads to charity,
not self-absorption and paralysis in doing good works.

reflection

Imagine a circle traced on the ground, and in its center a tree
sprouting with a shoot grafted into its side. The tree finds its
nourishment in the soil within the expanse of the circle, but
uprooted from the soil it would die fruitless. So think of the soul
as a tree made for love and living only by love. Indeed, without
this divine love, which is true and perfect charity, death would be
her fruit instead of life. The circle in which this tree's root, the
soul's love, must grow is true knowledge of herself, knowledge

that is joined to me, who like the circle has neither beginning nor end. You can go round and round within this circle, finding neither end nor beginning, yet never leaving the circle. This knowledge of yourself, and of me within yourself, is grounded in the soil of true humility, which is as great as the expanse of the circle (which is the knowledge of yourself united with me, as I have said). But if your knowledge of yourself were isolated from me, there would be no full circle at all. Instead, there would be a beginning in self-knowledge, but apart from me it would end in confusion.

So the tree of charity is nurtured in humility and branches out in true discernment. The marrow of the tree (that is, loving charity within the soul) is patience, a sure sign that I am in her and that she is united with me.[3]

chapter six

JOHN OF THE CROSS, PRISONER OF LOVE (1542–1591)

One of the greatest mystical poems was written in prison by a Carmelite priest whom we know today as Saint John of the Cross. The year was 1578, and the prison was in Toledo, the famed Spanish city whose images the great painter El Greco has seared into our mind's eye. Dark and forbidding is the city of Toledo in the paintings of El Greco.

There is an El Greco painting in the Cincinnati Art Museum entitled "Christ on the Cross with a View of Toledo." Dark are its hills, dark the city, dark the clouds—all in the background, except for streaks of light that are the color of the crucified Christ in the foreground, his elongated body dominating the canvas. Christ's head is tilted heavenward, his eyes rapt in contemplation.

The cross itself seems at first to be superimposed on a hostile landscape, or more accurately, cityscape, whose only light is the light it shares with the crucified figure that is its icon. The cross is planted in a foregrounded hillside, reminiscent of Calvary. Because of El Greco's use of light, the figure of Christ seems to wear the color of the city buildings, their only redeeming feature in the dark stormy landscape.

When I contemplate this painting of Christ on the cross, it seems oddly to be the Christ of Saint John's personal dark night, a prisoner somewhere in those cold forbidding buildings. There, betrayed by some of his own brothers who opposed the reforms he had initiated in the Carmelite way of life, John was confined for nine months in a room measuring six by ten feet, except for brief excursions to the refectory from time to time where he was flogged, kept on a diet of bread and water and then returned to solitary confinement. He did not complain or curse his tormentors. He entered instead into that dark night illu-mined by a light he could not see, which seemed to him as dark black as the night within his prison cell.

From December 3, 1577, to August, 1578, he surrendered to the darkness and let its hidden light purge his soul. He wrote poems that became his "Spiritual Canticle." In August he miraculously escaped and was sheltered by Teresa of Avila's nuns in Toledo. Like the elon-gated, stretched figure of Christ, John had been stretched by his expe-rience in prison, and he recorded that stretching for posterity.

John wrote the stanzas of his poem "The Dark Night" and those of "The Spiritual Canticle," and he wrote lengthy prose explications of both. They explain where the light is coming from on the body of El Greco's crucified. There is no light in the sky, except small light-gray cracks here and there. The light comes from within as John explains in the dark night.

In the painting, the light of that terrible journey breaks through the skin of Christ suffused with a flesh tone that is but a lightening of the dark sky and of the dark folds of Christ's skin. He is transformed into a lithe upward-winging man who seems to be metamorphosing into an angelic figure—except for the twisted legs and arms. The light shines through but not brightly or gaudily. It is revealed only in the sense that the man's flesh can be seen as the flesh of a man because of a light coming from somewhere other than the sun.

Christ is becoming a man illumined, the illumination being solely his manhood visible because of the light he himself has become. This is the light of Saint John's dark night, as it reveals itself in the person who has undergone divine illumination. Even the dark folds of Christ's flesh seem ready to unfold, their flesh colors suffused with the same inner light.

The cross in the painting is made of straight, well-cut planks; the figure on the cross is twisted, not by the cross, but by the struggle between light and darkness, the very struggle stretching the figure, twisting it into a graceful, almost flame-like elegance. There is, at this point of Christ's emergence, no pain, no blood, except for the dull, dried blood in the hands and feet. And there is no wound in the side! He is, as it were, already rising. Or better perhaps, emerging, for under the left armpit, there is what looks like a peeling back of the sky as of a black piece of paper, so that Christ seems to be emerging out of that black sky, his emergence tearing open and peeling back the blackness.

That Christ has no wound in his side says that this is not the Christ wounded from without by a soldier's spear; this is the Christ who has endured and is emerging from his own dark night, the mystical Christ, wounded and now emerging from an inner wound of abandonment by his Father that seemed all darkness but is the light that illumines his own transfigured body. The terrible black sky is only the dark canvas in which this mystical figure is imprisoned. His emergence is the only light the city of Toledo reflects—dully—but it does partake of this light of Christ.

As this great painting is an image, so are the poems of John images of the inner experience they try to replicate, or more accurately, approximate. They are only images, but in John and El Greco, the reader or viewer senses both men have "been there," that theirs are mystical souls. In this particular painting El Greco seems to be paint- ing the crucified Christ not on a white canvas, but on a canvas already painted pitch black and then releasing landscape, city, the crucified one and other figures, from within the blackness.

In John's poem "The Dark Night," the images begin with the lines, "*En una noche obscura*," a phrase difficult to render in English, espe- cially the word, "obscura." The phrase has been variously translated, "On a dark night," "One dark night," "Once in the dark of night," but always there's the word *dark* for *obscura*, a layered and rich word that contains the English word *obscure*. As it is difficult and never wholly satisfactory to translate a poem from one language to another, so the very Spanish words and images of John are an inadequate translation of the experience itself. All is approximation. But how else can one express the inexpressible except by words and images and metaphors that are at best but indirections, hints of what one sees in an instant that changes one's life?

I wonder, when I pray with this painting, if El Greco had read

John's, "Dark Night"? Or had he seen John's own painting of the crucifixion made famous by Salvador Dali? Or does El Greco's painting derive from something he himself had experienced in his own soul, or is the inner light of this painting something the old master learned as a young man painting icons in Greece? Whatever the case, I'm drawn to this painting; I always end up looking at it, no matter what else I've come to the museum to see. And I can never just look at the painting; it draws me in; it invites contemplation.

John's imprisonment, in its dark details, was an archetypal image of the interior struggle he named the dark night of the soul. The poems that issued from his own dark night, "The Dark Night" and "The Spiritual Canticle," are both full of light, though one is named dark; and therein is the core of John's mystical journey and his spiritual teaching.

The paradox lies in the fact that John's "The Dark Night" is as much light as is the light of his "Canticle." He says that the dark night is really an "inflow" of God into the soul, but it is an inflow that purges us of our natural and spiritual ignorance and imperfections. The dark night is really infused light, but the imperfect soul neither knows nor understands what is happening. This is so because up to this time the soul has been intensely engaged in striving to prepare itself for God's grace. Then, when God's infused contemplation arrives, the soul is blind to see that now God is at work, and what appears to be darkness is really light so bright that it blinds our seeing. John compares trying to see this infused contemplation to trying to look into the sun. God is working deep within, and because there are still impurities and baseness within, the light is so painful that it doesn't seem like light but darkness. In other words, if we are not yet entirely illumined, this light causes spiritual blindness, darkness.

In addition, when this light enters the soul, the soul feels unclean, and God seems to be against the very person the light is entering. The person suffers because it seems that God has abandoned him altogether; whereas just the opposite is happening, and it will take time for the person to adjust to this new light and be able to see what is really happening in this "dark" illumination.

God's mystical light, while seeming to impoverish the soul of its natural affections and possessions, is in reality preparing one to be able to enjoy fully all earthly and heavenly things with a divine freedom from attachment to them. In John, as in all mystics, to be pure and completely open before God is the purpose of the dark night, of living in darkness—*but* in order, then, to see the light and to see *by* that same light. Seeing by means of that infused Divine Light is what contemplation is.

John, because he is a poet, sees by means of metaphors that are themselves seen by the divine light he has come to see by. They are metaphors of intimacy with the divine lover, whom John portrays in the Canticle as a stag who has wounded him.

1. Where have you hidden,

Beloved, and left me moaning?

You fled like the stag

After wounding me;

I went out calling to you, and you were gone.[1]

....

9. Why, since you wounded

This heart, don't you heal it?

And why, since you stole it from me,

Do you leave it so,

And fail to carry off what you have stolen?[2]

11. Reveal your presence,

And may the vision of your beauty be my death,

For the sickness of love

Is not cured

Except by your very presence and image.[3]

And Christ, the Bridegroom, answers, calling the soul first a dove and then a bride.

Return, dove,

The wounded stag

Is in sight on the hill,

Cooled by the breeze of your flight.[4]

22. The bride has entered

The sweet garden of her desire,

And she rests in delight,

Laying her neck

On the gentle arm of her beloved[5]

23. Beneath the apple tree:

There I took you for my own,

There I offered you my hand,

And restored you,

Where your mother was corrupted.[6]

The language here is charged with ecstatic lovemaking. The soul as feminine bride is wounded by the entry of God into her inmost being. It is a transport beautifully rendered by Bernini in his statue "Saint Teresa in Ecstasy." So sensual, so sexual, is this marble rendering that some Victorians, on seeing it for first time, proclaimed it obscene, or at least indelicate.

To read John of the Cross is to enter into the world of ecstatic intimacy with God, who alone can satisfy the longings of the soul. It is an ecstasy bought for the dear price of purgation and illumination that feels like darkness, of a light that feels like darkness, of God's way that turns upside down one's habitual way of seeing things and living one's life. It involves the gospel paradox of the seed entering the dark earth and dying in order to grow, of losing one's life in order to find it, of selling all one's possessions in order to possess everything, of taking up the cross in order to rise from its crossed arms into heaven. This intimacy is effected by divine contemplation infused into the soul that has embarked upon the way of paradox by trying to live Christ's Sermon on the Mount.

Through one's own effort, on the one hand, and God's infused contemplation, on the other, the mystic has been shown a center within where God dwells in intimate union with the soul, and where, if the mystic responds to what he or she has been shown, a peace settles in the soul that remains despite the rhythm of trust and betrayal, guilt and forgiveness that every life is about.

Jesus complains of our having eyes but not seeing and having ears that don't really hear. The contemplation that results from the dark night of the soul gives us eyes that see and ears that hear divinely. John expresses this phenomenon with the words:

> 36. Let us rejoice, beloved,
>
> And let us go forth to behold ourselves in your beauty,
>
> To the mountain and to the hill,
>
> To where the pure water flows,
>
> And further, deep in the thicket.[7]

We will see ourselves in Christ's beauty, and we will see Christ's beauty everywhere. It is a gift to see this way, to experience,

> 39. The breathing of the air,
>
> The song of the sweet nightingale,
>
> The grove and its living beauty
>
> In the serene night,
>
> With a flame that is consuming and painless.[8]

All of these stanzas Saint John of the Cross painstakingly explicates, as he does the stanzas of "The Dark Night." These commentaries form the bulk of both "The Dark Night" and "The Spiritual Canticle" and were written at the request of others who wanted to know more specifically what the metaphors and images of the poem referred to in the inner life. One must read these commentaries carefully and prayerfully, for they are as dense and at times as complicated as the poems are transparent and simple in their images. The prose explications are John the spiritual theologian and doctor of the church writing; the poems are the lover and mystic searching for metaphors that incarnate his intimate experiences of God. They are the songs of the lover.

I prefer the poems to the prose because metaphor opens up infinite possibilities of readings and response that prose circumscribes with the author's own interpretation. The poems are for me the experiences themselves; the prose is the explanation of what they mean to the author. The poems open up my own experiences; the prose tells me what the poems open up for the author.

It is much more congenial and exciting for me to let the poems suggest and trigger similar longings, experiences and intimacies that in turn find their own metaphors. Perhaps that is only my own penchant for poetry, but I think it has also to do with the very nature of poetry, which by means of image, metaphor and sound says more than it says, denotes one thing and connotes another. As a rabbi friend once said to me, "Poetry is God-talk; theology is human-talk."

In one sense, it is amazing that John explains his own poem; poets usually do not do that, preferring to let the poem stand as it is, its own statement being the best and only articulation of what the poem is saying. But John is more than a poet. He is a humble guide of souls who realizes not everyone is equipped to read poetry, that many cannot relate to poetry, and his priestly soul wants to help others on their journey to God. He has written his own God-experience in his poems. Those who can read them will, and for those who can't he will lead through the poems by means of a step-by-step explication of what the metaphors and images and sounds of the poems refer to regarding the relationship of God to the soul.

No reading of a mystic, of course, substitutes for one's own encounter with God, one's own spiritual journey. But having embarked on that journey, one finds in John of the Cross a companion and guide who understands what one is suffering and experiencing, a guide who gives encouragement along the way that what one is undergoing is a series of passages that seem dark but lead to Divine enlightenment and union with God. He counsels perseverance through what the novice believes is a dark night that will never end, a dark night in which there is no light, nor ever will be.

With John as a guide, one feels that the darkness is not forever, that this darkness is indeed light. It is a light that will be revealed at last, a divine light by which one will see all things anew. That, in the end, is contemplation.

Even a brief summary of the life of John of the Cross shows graphically that, like Francis and Catherine, he was not simply a starry-eyed mystic, but a person of intense apostolic activity. Juan de Yepes, the youngest son of Gonzalo de Yepes and Catalina Alvarez, was born in 1542 in Fontiveros in Old Castille, Spain. When Juan was just three, his father died, and the family, already poor silk weavers, were left with no means of support. In order to provide for her two sons, Catalina soon moved the family to Medina del Campo, one of Spain's market cities. There, Juan, at the age of nine, entered a school for poor children, where he proved to be a good and diligent student. But when he was apprenticed to an artisan, he seemed unable to learn the trade. The governor of the hospital in Medina then took him into his service and Juan soon showed a gift for nursing and hospital work. When he had a chance to study at a nearby Jesuit school, he again excelled as a student. He studied the classics at night after his hospital work and, encouraged by the Jesuits, he began to study literature and write poetry.

He entered the Carmelite novitiate when he was twenty-one, after which he spent four years studying philosophy and theology at the University of Salamanca. His extensive study of the Bible is evident from the profuse biblical quotations and allusions in his writings. In 1568 he took his final vows as Juan de la Cruz, John of the Cross. He was already strongly drawn to the contemplative life and was thinking seriously about joining the Carthusians, where he would have more silence and solitude. But when he returned to Medina to say his first Mass, he met an extraordinary Carmelite nun, Teresa of Avila. Teresa was then past fifty—John was just twenty-seven—and she persuaded him to join in the reform of the Carmelite Order. Both John and Teresa were skilled organizers and doers, and together they founded the Discalced Carmelites, so called because Teresa's nuns, especially, went barefoot as a sign of radical commitment to Christ.

With two companions, an ex-prior and a lay brother, John inaugurated the reform among the friars on November 28, 1568. John became the first novice-master and laid the foundations of the reform. He held various posts in the reform until Teresa called him to Avila as director and confessor to the convent of the Incarnation, where she was prioress. He remained there for five years while the reform was spreading rapidly, though not without conflicts. Confusion arose over orders issued by the general chapter of the Carmelite Order and the apostolic nuncio. When John refused his general minister's order to return to Medina because he held his office from the apostolic nuncio and not the Carmelite chapter, he was accused of violating his vow of obedience. On December 3, 1577, he was blindfolded, arrested and imprisoned in a priory in Toledo.

He remained in prison for nine months, until by twisting strips of a blanket and tunic into a rope, he was able to escape from his high prison window. He was harbored and protected by the nuns of one of Teresa's convents.

He spent the following spring in a mountain hermitage in Andalusia, where he completed the composition of "The Dark Night" and "The Spiritual Canticle," which he had begun in prison. During the following years he was intensely occupied with the foundation and government of monasteries at Baeza, Granada, Cordova, Segovia and elsewhere. In 1582 he went to Granada as prior for three relatively quiet years. On a hillside not far from Alhambra, he wrote his commentaries on the poems.

On October 4, 1582, Teresa died and the order split into the Moderates and the Zelanti. John supported the Moderates, but the Zelanti won out and gained control of the Order. For a few years John remained in his position as vicar general of Andalusia and traveled widely by burro through southern Spain, going as far as Madrid and even to Lisbon, Portugal. He often slept in the open air or beside loud, overcrowded inns.

In 1588 he became prior at Segovia just as new disputes and dangers were breaking out in the Order. The government of the Order was changed, concentrating all power in the hands of a permanent committee that John resisted. When John also supported the nuns' endeavor to secure papal approbation of their constitutions, he incurred the displeasure of his superior who deprived John of his offices and sent him to one of the poorest monasteries in a remote area of Andalusia. Even there, though, he was the object of the resentment of two friars who were trying to have him expelled from the Order.

Only a final illness saved John from further persecution. He came down with a fever and an inflammation of his leg so serious that he traveled to the town of Ubeda, where he could receive medical attention. His disease, which was diagnosed as erysipelas, continued to worsen, and at midnight, December 14, 1591, as he was reciting aloud the psalm, "Into your hands, O Lord, I commend my spirit," John of the Cross died. Almost immediately there were popular demonstrations proclaiming his holiness. He was beatified in 1675 and canonized in 1726, receiving the title "Patron of the Afflicted" because of his Christlike handling of his own personal suffering and for his care for others. In 1926 he was declared a doctor of the church.

reflection

This dark night is an inflow of God into the soul that purges it of its habitual ignorances and imperfections, natural and supernatural, and which contemplatives call infused contemplation or mystical theology....God teaches the soul secretly and instructs it in the perfection of love without its doing anything or understanding how this happens.... Why, if it is a divine light...does one call it a dark night?...First, because of the height of the divine wisdom, which exceeds the capacity of the soul. Second, because of the soul's baseness and impurity; and on this account the wisdom is painful, afflictive, and also, dark for the soul.... Hence when the divine light of contemplation strikes souls not entirely illumined, it causes spiritual darkness.[9]

chapter seven

THÉRÈSE OF LISIEUX, THE LITTLE WAY (1873–1897)

Saint Thérèse of Lisieux was at heart an anti-mystic who said that she did not want to see God on earth; she preferred to live in faith. That is what her short life was all about, a life of faith marked by an extraordinary love that she came to see was her vocation.

It was a vocation that reached out to others from a small Carmelite cloister in a small town in Normandy, France, until she was beloved throughout the world for the countless miracles worked through her intercession and for her autobiography, *The Story of a Soul*, which is really three books in one.

Chapters one to eight were written at the request of her prioress, her oldest sister Pauline, who had preceded Thérèse into Carmel. Pauline and Marie, Thérèse's second-oldest sister and also a nun of Carmel, decided after the death of their beloved father to ask Thérèse to write down her memories of the early years of their family. Thérèse completed the manuscript in January, 1896, and gave it to Pauline.

The second part of the book is a letter to her sister Marie written at the latter's request when Thérèse was already gravely ill with tuberculosis and knew she hadn't long to live. In the letter she explains her particular vocation, her "Little Way" that has become so famous throughout the world.

The third manuscript was written at the request of Mother Marie de Gonzague, who had been prioress for seven three-year terms before Pauline, and who succeeded Pauline again after her term. Thérèse began her manuscript the very next morning, working two hours a day for as long as her strength allowed. The manuscript, understandably, is only about one-third as long as the first.

When *The Story of a Soul* was published, just a year after Thérèse's death, the arbitrary and domineering Mother Marie de Gonzague insisted the three manuscripts be combined so that the whole book would seem to be addressed to her—a move that hints at how Mother Marie herself must have been a significant part of the spiritual martyrdom Thérèse suffered at Carmel.

This genesis and structure of the book helps us to understand why the early part of the book is full of sentimentality and is marked by a cloying preciousness of style. It was written for her sisters, Pauline and Marie, and was never intended for a wider audience. In the later writing she thought she was writing simply to give Mother Marie de Gonzague the information she needed for her obituary.

But the book did reach a wider audience, becoming an international best-seller that touched millions of lives. For, embedded in Thérèse's almost schoolgirlish diction is an extraordinary love story that readers intuitively grasped. Here was no plaster-pretty saint, no sweet little woman that her image became in countless holy cards and sentimental statues. Here was a soul on fire with love of God, a love that endured incredible pain and suffering, even while experiencing a terrifying dark night of the soul.

Before her profession of vows, Christ her bridegroom had asked Thérèse what land she wanted to travel to and by what path. Thérèse answered, "The mountain of love," and Jesus could choose the way.

> And our Lord took me by the hand and made me enter a subterranean way where it is neither cold nor warm, where the sun does not shine and where rain and wind may not enter; a tunnel where I see nothing but a half-veiled glow from the downcast eyes in the face of my spouse... I gladly consent to spend my entire life in this underground darkness to which he has led me; my only wish is that my gloom will bring light to sinners.[1]

Such a request would surely seem like masochism were it not for Thérèse's joyful consent and those final words: "that my gloom will bring light to sinners." Hers is a sacrificial love that enters into the redemptive love of Jesus. One thinks of the words of Saint Paul, "I am now rejoicing in my sufferings for your sake, and in my flesh I am completing what is lacking in Christ's afflictions for the sake of his body, that is, the church" (Colossians 1:24).

Paul's words suggest that we, as the body of Christ, complete what Christ, the head of the body, began. Together with Christ we make the body of the church whole by our own joyful sacrifices of love. That certainly was what Thérèse believed, and that is the motivation of her little subterranean way of darkness and faith that began, even before she was born, with the deep piety of her parents.

Marie-Francoise-Thérèse Martin was born January 2, 1873, in Alençon, a French city famous for its lace. She was the fifth daughter and last child of Louis Martin and Zelie Guiren, who was forty-two and already ill (probably with the breast cancer that she died from four-and-a-half years later) when Thérèse was born. Both she and her husband had tried to enter religious life, but were turned down—Louis because he wanted to become a priest and did not know Latin, and Zelie for reasons that are unknown. But when Zelie could not become a nun, she vowed to bring children into the world for God.

Louis was a watchmaker and jeweler, an idealistic dreamer and impractical man who eventually abandoned his profession to assist Zelie in her lucrative lace business, which employed several other women. Both were extremely devout and attended the earliest Mass every day. Though Zelie had vowed to have children for God, the couple was celibate the first ten months of their marriage because of Louis's reservations about sexual relations. These were finally overcome through the intervention of their spiritual director, and they had nine children. Two boys and two girls died in infancy, and they were left with five daughters.

Pauline was the oldest of the girls. Then followed Marie, Leonie (the only one who did not enter the convent), Celine and Thérèse, who was the much doted-on and pampered darling of the family—her mother's favorite, as is evident from her letters to Pauline away at boarding school. At first it looked like Thérèse, too, would die in infancy, but soon after her birth she was sent to a wet-nurse in the country for a year and was returned healthy and vivacious and not a little stubborn and self-willed. "Little Thérèse," her mother wrote, "is going to be wonderfully good; the germ of goodness can already be seen." Although, "She is such a little madcap...not nearly so docile as her sister. When she says 'no' nothing can make her change, and she can be terribly obstinate. You could keep her down in the cellar all day without getting a 'yes' out of her; she would rather sleep there."[2]

When Zelie died, Thérèse was just four, and the trauma of that parting sent her into extreme grief that became pathological, marked by hallucinations and seizures compounded by terrible headaches when her sister and surrogate mother Pauline left to enter Carmel five years later.

Then an extraordinary thing happened when Thérèse was ten years old; she was cured by something the family considered a miracle, one of the few recorded visions in Thérèse's life. While they were praying together before the statue of the Blessed Virgin Mary, Thérèse saw Our Lady smile at her and heard Mary's assuring words that Thérèse delighted her and that one day she would take Thérèse in her arms in heaven because Mary herself had now become her mother.

Shortly after the death of Zelie, the family had moved to Lisieux in order to leave painful memories behind them and because of Louis's concern about the worldliness of his children's playmates and relatives in Alençon. The two older girls, Pauline, seventeen, and Marie, sixteen, had become the surrogate parents of the two youngest, Thérèse going to Pauline and Celine to Marie, until Pauline entered Carmel and Marie took charge of both girls. Though Thérèse was cured of her nervous disorder by her vision of the Blessed Virgin, she soon had to endure another trial, that of scrupulosity, accusing herself of countless sins that she felt obliged to confess incessantly. Marie took charge of the situation and told her not only how many sins she could confess but which imaginary sins she was allowed to confess.

This period of scrupulosity was a terrible time for Thérèse, who was trying beyond her years to be a saint and was becoming more and more self-preoccupied with her spiritual progress. As she wrote in *Story of a Soul,*

> One would have to pass through this martyrdom to understand it well.... All my most simple thoughts and actions became the cause of trouble for me, and I had relief only when I told them to Marie. This cost me dearly, for I believed I was obliged to tell her the absurd thoughts I had even about her. As soon as I laid down my burden, I experienced peace for an instant; but this peace passed away like a lightning-flash, and soon my martyrdom began over again.[3]

This passage is one of the reasons *Story of a Soul* meant so much to me as a young seminarian of fourteen. Thérèse, the great saint, had once suffered the scrupulosity I was suffering, which didn't pass from me until four years later when I entered the novitiate, and a prolonged period of aridity ensued that brought home to me the truth that nothing really depends solely on us; everything is God's gift, and we cannot force our own holiness by self-preoccupation or exaggerated penances or prolonged prayers. My own scrupulosity, as it often is, was really self-will in a pious camouflage, a misdirected obsession with being holy.

Thérèse realized as much on Christmas Eve when she was thirteen. The family tradition was that the children would find their shoes filled with candy and gifts when they returned from Midnight Mass.

Though Thérèse was really too old for this, they still carried on the tradition for her. As she was running up the stairs to take off her coat, she heard her father say to Celine that he hoped this would be the last year for this sort of thing. He sounded put out, and Thérèse was mortified and thought that if she went down just then, she would cry.

Instead, something happened to her, and she bounded down the stairs, made a grand fuss over the candy and presents to please her father. She had only put out her shoes for his sake in the first place, but she pretended to be thrilled with it all, because, as she wrote later, she'd been moved to come downstairs by charity, which Jesus had given her when all she wanted to do was cry. From then on she began to forget herself and to live to please others. "That night," Thérèse wrote, "began the third period of my life, the most beautiful and the most filled with graces from heaven."[4] The other two periods she mentions are from her birth to her mother's death, followed by a ten-year-long period of illness and anxiety.

Shortly afterward she resolved to follow her sisters into the Carmelite monastery of Lisieux. She had been aware of her vocation already when she was nine, but when she was fourteen, the divine call became insistent, and though in France the customary age for entering was twenty-one, she was determined to seek permission to enter. Pauline and Celine agreed, but Marie thought she was too young. Then there was the problem of her father. What would her entrance into Carmel do to him? But Thérèse worked up the courage to talk with Louis, who was sixty-three years old and had already suffered a stroke. Their talk convinced her father that Thérèse's vocation was real, and he agreed that she should seek an early entrance into the convent.

Then there was the prioress to consult. She agreed, but the father superior said no; the bishop, too, thought she should wait until she was twenty-one. Thérèse, though, was undeterred and determined to travel to Rome with her father to speak to Pope Leo XIII. Thérèse's persuasive powers being what they were, in the fall of 1887, she, Celine and their father journeyed to Rome on "pilgrimage," her real purpose being to ask the pope for early entrance into Carmel.

Seeing in the public papal audience her opportunity to speak with the pope, Thérèse, surprising the pope and everyone in attendance, threw herself at the feet of the Holy Father and made her request to enter the cloister of Carmel at the age of fifteen. Pope Leo, taken aback and caught off guard, uttered the disappointing generality, "Go...go.... You will enter if God wills it."[5]

Thérèse, crestfallen, had no choice but to return to Lisieux empty-handed. However, the mother superior had been working on the bishop behind the scenes and, on New Year's Day, Thérèse received a letter confirming that the bishop had given his permission—but not immediately. Thérèse was to wait until after Lent; she would be received on March 9, 1888. She wrote later of her entrance: "My soul experienced a peace so sweet, so deep, it would be impossible to express it."[6]

In Carmel she took the name Thérèse of the Child Jesus and gradually transformed her ideals of being a missionary, or a martyr like Joan of Arc, into her "Little Way," a spirituality of attention to the smallest details of life as the locus of virtue. Even the smallest of deeds done for love of God grew large in its potential to reveal the face of God. Not that all of Thérèse's deeds were small, even from a human standpoint. She determined to embrace her sisters in religion cheerfully, a not so small task; for despite the goodness of the nuns, Thérèse's commitment meant putting up with the inevitable pettiness and jealousies, the small-mindedness and resentments of a rather Jansenistic convent in nineteenth-century Normandy.

When she was appointed novice mistress, Thérèse did not shrink from the difficult task of spiritual correction and sacrificing for the novices. She became an extraordinary director of souls, and that once again demanded much of her, much letting go, much trust in God, as in these paragraphs from her *Story of a Soul:*

> The moment I began to deal with souls I realized instantly that the task was beyond my strength. I put myself quickly in the arms of God and behaved like babies who when frightened bury their heads on their fathers' shoulders. I said: "Lord, You see that I am too little to feed Your children. Put food into my hand if it is through me that You want to give each of them what is good for her. Without leaving Your arms and without even turning my head, I will distribute Your treasure to all the souls who come to ask me for food....
>
> I know it seems easy to help souls, to make them love God above all, and to mould them according to His will. But actually, without His help it is easier to make the sun shine at night. One must banish one's own tastes and personal ideas and guide souls along the special way Jesus indicates for them rather than along one's own particular way....
>
> God has given me the grace of having no fear of a fight. I will do my duty at any cost. More than once I have been told: "If you

want to succeed with me, severity is of no use. You will get nowhere unless you are gentle." But I know that no one is a good judge in his own case. If a surgeon performs a painful operation on a child, the child will scream and say that the cure is worse than the disease. But after a few days when he is cured, he is delighted to be able to run about and play. It is exactly the same where souls are concerned. They soon realize that a little bitterness is better than sweetness.[7]

So much for the image of Saint Thérèse as the pious, trembling "Little Flower," or the pious child hiding in the bosom of her mother, then in the bosom of the family of doting father and sisters.

Thérèse lived less than ten years in Carmel, having contracted tuberculosis soon after entering the cloister and suffering without complaint the consequences of the disease in a dark and drafty, poorly heated convent. When she died in 1897 at age twenty-four, seven years after taking her final vows, she left behind more writings than did John of the Cross, another Carmelite who was twice her age when he died. But she left behind something even more: She said that she would spend her heaven doing good on earth, and that is precisely what she has done. "Thus you will know them by their fruits," Jesus says (Matthew 7:20). How well we know the holiness of this great saint; her fruits have been good and plentiful.

Thérèse was canonized by Pope Pius XI in 1925, a thousand letters a day having arrived at the Vatican attesting to miracles worked through her intercession. Pope John Paul II declared her a doctor of the church in 1997, the third woman (Teresa of Avila and Catherine of Siena being the other two) and the thirty-third saint to be honored as such.

How, then, is this saint of small things, who left us her "Little Way," a mystic? We've already mentioned her vision of the Blessed Virgin Mary smiling on her when she was but a child, and she wrote of another vision she had when she was fourteen years old.

> One Sunday when I was looking at a picture of Our Lord on the Cross, I saw the Blood coming from one of His hands, and I felt terribly sad to think that It was falling to the earth and that no one was rushing forward to catch It. I determined to stay continually at the foot of the Cross and receive It. I knew that I should then have to spread It among other souls. The cry of Jesus on the Cross—"I am thirsty"—rang continually in my heart and set me burning with a new, intense longing. I wanted to quench the thirst of my Well-Beloved and I myself was consumed with a thirst for souls. I was concerned not with the souls of priests but with those of great sinners which I wanted to snatch from the flames of hell."[8]

Such visions are rare for Thérèse; hers is not the way of visions and ecstasy. Hers is the Little Way, which is entering into the love of God and doing everything, no matter how small, for the love of God. Her mysticism (and all mysticism, in one sense) is simply an intensification of the Christian life, a gift of God that reveals the mystery of baptism and the paschal mystery to one's mind and heart, sometimes to one's physical eyes and ears, as well. The mystical experience, instead of being a discrete kind of Christian experience, is really a revelation of the mystery all Christians live and is the result of an intense commitment to and living of the baptismal mystery of dying to sin and rising with Christ into his mystical body, the church.

Such a mysticism is not all the sweetness and light that is so often associated with Saint Thérèse because of the first eight chapters of her *Story of a Soul*, where she recounts her childhood and their childhood together for her sisters. The real *Saint* Thérèse is revealed in her sense of a loss of intimacy with Jesus toward the end of her brief life, which elicits this anguished outpouring:

> Then suddenly the fog which surrounds me becomes dense: it penetrates my soul and envelops it in such a way that it is impossible to discover within it the sweet image of my Fatherland; everything has disappeared! When I want to rest my heart fatigued by the darkness which surrounds it by the memory of the luminous country after which I aspire, my torment redoubles; it seems to me that the darkness, borrowing the voice of sinners, says mockingly to me: "You are dreaming about the light, about a fatherland embalmed in the sweetest perfumes; you are dreaming about the eternal possession of the Creator of all these marvels; you believe that one day you will walk out of this fog which surrounds you! Advance, advance; rejoice in death which will give you not what you hope for but a night still more profound, the night of nothingness."
>
> [But] in spite of this trial which has taken away *all my joy*, I can nevertheless cry out: "You have given me DELIGHT, O Lord, in ALL your doings." For is there a joy greater than that of suffering out of love for You? The more interior the suffering is and the less apparent to the eyes of creatures, the more it rejoices You, O my God! But if my suffering was really unknown to You, which is

impossible, I would still be happy to have it, if through it I could prevent or make reparation for one single sin against faith....

When I sing of the happiness of heaven, and of the eternal possession of God, I feel no joy in this, for I simply sing what I WANT TO BELIEVE. It is true that at times a very small ray of the sun comes to illumine the darkness, and then the trial ceases for an instant, but afterwards the memory of this ray, instead of causing me joy, makes my darkness even more dense.[9]

In this long quote is Thérèse the doctor of the church, Thérèse the missionary saint, Thérèse of the Little Way, Thérèse the younger sister writing to her abbess, who is her "mother" in religious life, Thérèse the mystic who lives for and in the love of Jesus, whose absence has left her in the dark night of the soul, which is the most excruciating trial the mystic has to confront and embrace.

What, then, does Saint Thérèse, the doctor of the church, teach us? Mainly, it is this: Christian mysticism is not an esoteric branch of theology or something separate from the gospel life. It *is* the gospel life lived more intensely because of an intimate experience of God that has transformed the believer into open ground for the seed of God, a receptive womb for the impregnation of the Holy Spirit. The believer conceives and brings forth Christ anew in his or her own life.

One does not flee the daily humanness of life to ascend to some rarefied spiritual stratosphere or world of ideas or ecstasy. One waits like Mary, God's mother, for the impregnation of the Holy Spirit, one receives and responds and brings forth in one's life the God who is conceived in prayer, who grows in the womb of the soul, and is born into the world through one's acts of virtue that derive from the self that has been transformed by conceiving, bearing and giving birth to God.

For Thérèse this transformation takes place through what she calls the "Little Way," whose fruit she expresses in these words:

> After earth's exile, I hope to go and enjoy You in the Fatherland, but I do not want to lay up merits for heaven. I want to work for *Your Love alone....*
>
> In the evening of this life, I shall appear before you with empty hands, for I do not ask You, Lord, to count my works. All our justice is stained in your eyes. I wish, then, to be clothed in your own *Justice* and to receive from your *Love* the eternal possession of *yourself.* [10]

In the end, all of us, like Saint Thérèse of Lisieux, come before God with empty hands. We have nothing to boast of, as Saint Paul says, except the cross of our Lord Jesus Christ. Yet we do not despair. For our very emptiness has made a space for God. What we perceive as our poverty is our richness.

If we come before God boasting of merit and virtue, we have no need of the mercy and love of God. We believe we have merited eternal life; we deserve heaven. So we believe. The truth is, no one deserves heaven, no one can merit eternal life. All is gift. God's grace is freely given. Virtue, therefore, is not the selfish, misguided storing up of merit for ourselves—that would be an action as selfish as sin. Rather, virtue is a response to the merciful love of God, who, as Saint Paul reminds us, loved us *before* we were virtuous, loved us when we were still in our sins.

What I am trying to say has much to do with focus, orientation. If *my* virtue is focused on *me*, on what *I* do, what *I* give up, what *I* sacrifice, then it is not virtue but veiled egotism. For if any true virtue can be attributed to me, it is the result of focusing, not on myself, but on God, responding to God's love, so that my orientation is ever on God and not on myself.

Jesus says there are really only two commandments, and all the other commandments are kept if we keep these two: To love the Lord our God with our whole soul and heart and mind, and to love our neighbor as ourselves. If our effort and our focus are on God and neighbor, then virtue becomes what happens to us in forgetting our own self-betterment and loving God and others. To love God wholeheartedly and our neighbor as we would prefer to love ourselves is to love ourselves and better ourselves.

When we've spent our lives loving God and others, there is a gradual self-emptying that becomes a filling up as well. We have nothing to offer but the empty hands of a Thérèse—empty because they've surrendered all they've held onto—and those empty hands become the resting place of God.

And that is the secret of Thérèse, her Little Way. Her hands are empty from giving and letting go, and God fills. That filling up with God is virtue. Virtue is not something she has; it is what she doesn't have because she's given all away. What we don't have is what we have; what we give away is what we keep. For in the gesture of surrender is the mystery of love, a love typified in Jesus' words from the cross, "Father, into your hands I commend my spirit" (Luke 23:46).

Jesus' own hands are nailed to the cross. He has no hands to reach out and give anymore. At that point the Father's hands take over. They receive his spirit; they become the hands of Jesus. In our surrender is the same dynamic. When love has brought us to the point of having nothing more to give, then God becomes our filling and our giving hands. That alone is virtue: that point at which God takes over and makes up in us what we no longer have in us to give. Giving leads to emptying, which leads to filling up with God.

The terrible emptying of Thérèse in the previous long quote of the dark night of the soul is the reason she could utter these beautiful last words a few seconds before she died: "Oh! I love Him!... My God.... I love You!" "Little Way indeed! Anything but little; it may be little in the acts, but huge in the performing and in the reward. It is the living out of the first few words of Jesus in his first sermon:

> Blessed are the poor in spirit, for theirs is the kingdom of heaven.
>
> Blessed are those who mourn, for they will be comforted.
>
> Blessed are the meek, for they will inherit the earth.
>
> Blessed are those who hunger and thirst for righteousness, for they will be filled.
>
> Blessed are the merciful, for they will receive mercy.
>
> Blessed are the pure in heart, for they will see God.
>
> (Matthew 5:3–8)

What Thérèse's Little Way shows us is that all these blessings of Jesus can be ours, no matter how small and insignificant we may consider our lives to be, if only we surrender every action of our lives to the love of God and try to do everything we do for the love of God. Thérèse is a doctor of a simple gospel way of living that doesn't even need to leave the confines of one's home. Even inside a small and dark convent in Normandy one can be transformed by Christ and transform the world with the smallest acts of love.

reflection

Prayer of Surrender in the Spirit of Saint Thérèse

Assume a position of prayer. Close your eyes and open your hands and surrender your life to God's mercy and love. You know what it is you need to surrender, but it is hard to let go of it. Don't be discouraged. The repeated handing-over to God in prayer will work its own miracle.

One way to effect this surrender is to repeat, as a mantra, your deepest desire. For example, "God, my God, I want to be filled with you." After each uttering of this mantra, pause and let whatever objections, reservations, qualifications and excuses rise to the surface of your consciousness. Then resume your mantra, "God, my God, I want to be filled with you." Repeat this process for as long as your prayer time lasts. Gradually, the negative responses will diminish, and you will be able to know things you could not know without letting God fill your mind; you will be able to do things you could not do without letting God fill your heart; you will be able to experience moral freedom in areas of your life that are now filling up with God that before were paralyzed by and imprisoned in pride, jealousy, lust, fear, sloth, gluttony or whatever debilitating illusion the hands of your soul were desperately reaching for, clinging to.

What is important is perseverance in the prayer and its gestures of surrender: real gestures like opening your hands, or symbolic gestures of opening your soul, or both, secure in what Saint Thérèse herself taught: that God is satisfied even with a look, or any other simple sign of love.

chapter eight

GERARD MANLEY HOPKINS, IMMORTAL DIAMOND (1844–1889)

Gerard Manley Hopkins is an old and trusted friend. I met him some fifty years ago when, as a newly professed friar and freshman in college, I read for the first time his extraordinary mystical poem, "God's Grandeur." The final lines still ring in my ear.

> There lives a dearest freshness deep down things;
> And though the last lights off the black West went
> Oh, morning, at the brown brink eastward, springs—
> Because the Holy Ghost over the bent
> World broods with warm breast and with ah! bright wings.[1]

That image of the Holy Ghost as a bird nestling the world with God's motherly love, God's comforting breast that will hatch the world anew in the light of the salvation contained in the bright wings that will lift the world heavenward, was such a consolation; it gave me hope despite everything negative we have done to the earth.

But it was not "God's Grandeur" that drew Hopkins to my heart. It was his so-called "Terrible Sonnets" that incarnated for me what I had been experiencing since entering the novitiate two years earlier. As a young boy and all through high school seminary I was filled with con-solation and a sense of the presence of Christ and his Mother Mary. Then, from the very day of donning the habit of Saint Francis on August 15 of the same year as my high school graduation, all of that sweetness and light ceased; I was left with myself only.

I can still vividly see myself sitting in the classroom of Duns Scotus College seminary and turning the page to the poem Father Leander, our English instructor, began to read aloud. It was Hopkins's sonnet that began, "I wake and feel the fell of dark, not day." The last six lines of this sonnet riveted me to the page:

> I am gall, I am heartburn. God's most deep decree
> Bitter would have me taste: my taste was me;
> Bones built in me, flesh filled, blood brimmed the curse.
> Selfyeast of spirit a dull dough sours. I see
> The lost are like this, and their scourge to be
> As I am mine, their sweating selves; but worse.[2]

Though I felt powerless to do anything about it—and that was the point—there it was on the page; and reading it, hearing it, I knew this was me. I'd not known before the power of poetry to recreate in words a feeling I thought was so individual to me. I didn't know anyone else felt like that, yet there were the words, there was the experience. There was the image: "Selfyeast of spirit a dull dough sours." Exactly. That is what I had been trying to do for over two years: selfyeast my already dull dough of a self. And sour was the taste, sour the smell. Only now I was not alone. Someone else was there. A Jesuit priest, dead since 1889, was alive and well in these words, or at least the words were alive and well and acting on a young Franciscan friar in 1957.

From then on the poems of Gerard Manley Hopkins, with all their complexity and densely layered syntax, became a sort of *vade mecum*. I carried them with me in a small Penguin paperback edited by W.H. Gardner. I read the poems. I tried to tease out the sense of the lines, their sound, their idiosyncratic style, their mystery. Poem after poem would yield lines that made present something I'd experienced or something I didn't know I knew, or some mystery, some glimpse of the divine that I'd almost see, almost grasp.

Here was a sacramental poet. For him everything seemed to be a sacrament of the presence of God; his words grasped the individuality of the thing that in turn revealed the Word that inhabited it. I knew even then, as a young man, that Hopkins was a mystical poet, an intimate of God whom he experienced through words that grasped God's unique incarnation in everything that is.

Each thing in its very uniqueness, which Hopkins calls *inscape*, reveals the unique word of God that it is. This inscape is elicited or revealed through an intuitive knowing that Hopkins calls *instress*. For him, as a poet, it is language itself that instresses an inscape. Language itself becomes the inscape of God, reveals God as the Word inside the word.

Through journals and letters, through sermons and especially through some of the greatest incarnational poems ever written in English, Hopkins tries to incarnate the Word (Christ) in the word (the

unique name) that is each thing. Words themselves become a sacrament of the real presence of God.

As with most Christian mystics, intimacy with Christ is the be-all
and end-all of Hopkins's life. And when his assurance of the presence
of Christ is shattered through a dark night of the soul in which he feels
abandoned by Christ, he writes his "Terrible Sonnets"; he endeavors
to instress the inscape of his depression, to know through language the
individual depression that is his.

Hopkins's words also internalize the world that becomes something more within him. His first great poetic outpouring was triggered
by the wreck, off the coast of England, of the German ship *Deutschland*.
Five Franciscan nuns, exiled from Germany by the Falk Laws (laws
against Catholics), were drowned in the storm. The event was internalized by Hopkins and becomes, in the words of the poem, the incarnation of Hopkins's own inner shipwreck in which Christ was and is
revealed.

The poem begins powerfully with:

> Thou mastering me
> God! giver of breath and bread;
> World's strand, sway of the sea;
> Lord of living and dead;
> Thou hast bound bones and veins in me, fastened me flesh,
> And after it almost unmade, what with dread,
> Thy doing: and dost thou touch me afresh?
> Over again I feel thy finger and find thee.[3]

With the enunciation of these lines, we know we are in the presence of
a great and original voice, a poet who is more than a poet, a poet who is

a mystic as well. Who, then, was this incredibly modern nineteenth-century poet?

Gerard Manley Hopkins was a Jesuit priest whose mysticism is evident in his life and in his poetry. When he died in Dublin on June 8, 1889, Hopkins was remembered only by his family and a few friends. The recognition and fame he has today did not begin until 1918 when his friend and poet laureate Robert Bridges published his poems. It was immediately evident that Hopkins was a creative genius. And in 1930 when a second edition of his poems appeared, the literary world realized that here was a Victorian who was a true modern. Here, too, was a startlingly original English voice.

Gerard Manley was born at Stratford, Essex, England, on July 28, 1844, the eldest of Manley Hopkins's and Kate Smith's nine children. His father, something of a poet himself, founded a marine insurance business and was for a time Hawaii's consul-general in London. Manley and Kate and their nine children were moderate Anglicans and shared a variety of talents in poetry, music and painting.

In 1852 the family moved to Hampstead, north of London, where Gerard Manley attended Highgate School until 1863 when he won a scholarship to Balliol College, Oxford. At Balliol, Hopkins continued to write passable verse, as he had from his early years, and he excelled in classics, becoming an outstanding classical scholar. When he was twenty-one, he underwent a moral and spiritual crisis that ended when he was received into the Roman Catholic church by John Henry Newman.

Two years later, after destroying most of his verse, he entered the Jesuit Novitiate at Roehampton, just outside London, and resolved to write no further verse unless asked to by his superiors. For almost seven years he concentrated wholly on philosophy and theology, and on the Spiritual Exercises of Saint Ignatius of Loyola, the basis of the Jesuit life and a profound influence on his later poetry. During this period Hopkins wrote only occasional verses in honor of Our Lady or to commemorate Jesuit community anniversaries.

Then, late in 1875, the news of the wreck of the *Deutschland* precipitated the end of Hopkins's poetic silence. The rector of Saint Beuno's College, South Wales, where Hopkins was studying theology, encouraged him to write something about the incident, and the result was the long poem "The Wreck of the Deutschland." It is filled with intense emotion and wrestles with God's ways with humans. It is a poem of power and movement mimetic of the very storm that destroyed the Franciscan nuns. The floodgates now open, Hopkins continued to write occasional lyrics, sonnets and deeply religious poems.

After ordination in 1877, little Father Hopkins—he was slightly over five feet tall—was sent to pastoral and teaching assignments in London, Liverpool, Glasgow, Oxford and, in 1882, to Stonyhurst College, Lancashire. He suffered bouts of ill health and, despite his brilliant mind, was never a successful preacher or teacher, as was his mentor, Cardinal Newman, of whom Matthew Arnold wrote, "Who could resist the charm of that spiritual apparition, gliding in the dim afternoon light through the aisles of St. Mary's, rising into the pulpit, and then in the most entrancing of voices breaking the silence with words and thought which were a religious movement, subtle, sweet, mournful."[4] Of Hopkins, however, one of his superiors remarked that his mind moved in "concentric circles," making it difficult to follow his thought, though he was, all the same, universally liked for his puckish humor, his gentleness and his holiness.

His last assignment was to University College, Dublin, as the chair of classics. There Hopkins suffered the same difficulties in teaching, despite his brilliant intellect and vast classical learning. Years later his students remembered his incredible thoroughness, recalling two-hour lectures that exhausted them (but not Hopkins's knowledge) on the Latin conjunction *atque* (and). His own recollections are filled with his interest in music and words, and with patterns like those formed by steam puffing from locomotives.

In the spring of 1889, Hopkins contracted typhoid fever, and despite medical intervention, peritonitis set in. His parents were summoned from England, and on June 8, after receiving the sacraments of the church, he died murmuring the words, "I am so happy, so happy."

And that would have been the end of it, despite the tributes in the press and in letters concerning, as Coventry Patmore put it, "the *authority* of his goodness."

But that was not the end of it, either for Hopkins now united with God, "beauty's gift and beauty's giver," or for his reputation, which skyrocketed after the publication of his poems almost thirty years later in 1918.

Unlike Catherine of Siena's, Gerard Manley Hopkins's life was the comparatively uneventful, predictable life of a priest-academic, a teacher who doesn't like to teach, a preacher whose sermons fail because of their dense language and circular thinking, a man whose frail health and proneness to depression made of him a wraithlike presence in the classroom and at the altar.

But his inner experience is just the opposite. It explodes with powerful transforming experiences that he incarnates in original and extraordinarily dynamic poems. Afterward, it is almost as if the ecstasy of his internalizing of the objects of creation leaves him exhausted as when a mystic emerges from an intense experience of God. His poems incarnate the dynamic presence of the Word in individual things. The words of the poems release God, who is hidden in each individual thing, through the right words in the right combinations. The words themselves incarnate the God who is incarnate already in the things the poems are "instressing."

The poems are Hopkins's real experience, which is an ongoing self-emptying, just as Christ emptied himself, becoming obedient even to death on a cross. As Christ is obedient to the word of the Father, and *is* the Word of the Father, so Hopkins becomes obedient to the Word revealed in things, then in turn empties himself of the possession of things so that he can hear the words they are. In emptying himself of words, the poet incarnates the word he is expressing. For words, like things, are the outstressing of the Blessed Trinity. In "selving," both words and things become the locus, the place of the selving God.

This must seem terribly convoluted and vague, and in a sense it is. But perhaps it is really something simple. Perhaps a mystical poet like Hopkins is simply trying to find words that become sacraments of the presence of God that the poet sees in all things. Everything is a sacrament (an external sign of an interior reality), and the poet tries to make words into sacraments in the same way. The words contain or incarnate the same God that the individual thing incarnates. As Hopkins puts it:

Each mortal thing does one thing and the same:

Deals out that being indoors each one dwells;

Selves—goes itself; *myself* it speaks and spells,

Crying *Whát I dó is me: for that I came.*

I say móre: the just man justices;

Keeps gráce: thát keeps all his going graces;

Acts in God's eye what in God's eye he is –

Christ—for Christ plays in ten thousand places,

Lovely in limbs, and lovely in eyes not his

To the Father through the features of men's faces.[5]

Hopkins's belief in the Real Presence of Christ in the Eucharist is central to understanding this sacramental vision. He saw Christ in the bread and wine; he saw the same Christ in all people and things. The words of the priest make present the unseen eucharistic Christ; the words of the poet reveal the same Christ hidden within everything that is.

Divine Presence consoles Hopkins, charges him with ecstatic words; Divine Presence withdrawn leaves him in deep depression with tortured words that reveal the futility of self-communion.

From the very beginning Hopkins was perceived as an eccentric and odd poet, especially as his friend Robert Bridges's erudite notes to the poems emphasized Hopkins's obscurity. But difficulty in idiom is not difficulty in thought, and once one grasps Hopkins's technique, the poems ring clear and simple and beautiful, especially when read aloud, as he intended. His vision is deep, his language accommodates and plumbs those depths.

No English poet has spoken so eloquently and powerfully of the mystical life as has Hopkins, beginning with his great outpouring "The Wreck of the Deutschland." The storm that destroyed the five nuns becomes an image of the storm within Hopkins as he wrestles with his first shattering vision of God, which he writes about in that poem of 1877. The storm outside precipitates another storm within, which struggles with where God is in the inner and outer storms of our lives, and who that God is.

Those who do not understand this deep religious sensibility fail to grasp Hopkins's poems, especially "The Wreck of the Deutschland" and the "Terrible Sonnets." The latter they see as poems of a depressed psyche, of a priest-poet whose priestly and poetic sensibilities are in conflict. In reality these sonnets are not about religion or priesthood or the poet's failure to measure up either as a poet or a priest, but they are about God and the soul and how our growth in God takes place when we think God is punishing us or abandoning us. Hopkins's focus in the sonnets and in "The Wreck of the Deutschland" is on God and his relationship with God, who seems to be manhandling him. But when he writes of these feelings about God, a new insight and vision emerges.

In the Carrion Comfort octave of the "Terrible Sonnets," for example, the poet addresses God:

> But ah, but O thou terrible, why wouldst thou rude on me
> Thy wring-world right foot rock? Lay a lionlimb against me? scan
> With darksome devouring eyes my bruisèd bones? and fan,
> O in turns of tempest, me heaped there; me frantic to avoid thee
> and flee?[6]

What an image of the terrible, mastering God! It is the same God of the first lines of "The Wreck of the Deutschland," who now rudely rocks the poet back and forth with the same huge foot he rocks the world with. And not gently, the way one rocks a cradle, but violently, rudely. Then God eyes his bruised bones and instead of relenting, comes in tempest with his winnowing fan to cleanse his floor of chaff although the poet is already crushed, frantically trying to get out of God's way.

But in the sestet of this sonnet, as there should be, there is a turn; and the poet understands why God is treating him so roughly.

Why? That my chaff might fly; my grain lie, sheer and clear.
Nay, in all that toil, that coil, since (seems) I kissed the rod,
Hand rather, my heart lo! lapped strength, stole joy, would laugh,
    chéer.
Cheer whom though? the hero whose heaven-handling flung me,
    foót tród
Me? or me that fought him? O which one? is it each one? That
    night, that year
Of now done darkness I wretch lay wrestling with (my God!) my
    God.[7]

The poet realizes that God's roughness and his own recoiling took joy once he submitted to God and kissed God's rough hand. He cheers not knowing whom to cheer—the hero-God or himself that fought him.

It is done darkness now; he is writing about a past experience in which he realizes now that he was wrestling with God. Whatever else he thought was happening at the time, in the poem he comes to the realization that it was all about God and him. And it was good and afterward brings joy, laughter and cheering of the two combatants.

For the mystic the relationship with God is everything and goes
through all the vicissitudes of every love relationship, from ecstasy to
hurting one another, to the temptation to despair, which is how this
poem begins:

Not, I'll not, carrion comfort, Despair, not feast on thee;

Not untwist—slack they may be—these last strands of man

In me ór, most weary, cry, I can no more. I can;

Can something, hope, wish day come, not choose not to be.[8]

What can he do? If nothing else, he cannot choose to not be. He'll not
kill himself. "To be or not to be," Hamlet says, "that is the question."
The poet answers that no matter what, he will be.

Compare this poem of the dark night of the soul with the poem of
ecstasy, "The Windhover: *To Christ Our Lord.*" It is Hopkins's most
mystically telling poem, much as the "Canticle" is John of the Cross's
quintessential mystical poem. Hopkins himself, in a letter to Robert
Bridges, says it's "the best thing I ever wrote." In this poem is the
inscape of Hopkins's mystical life, condensed and instressed.

Some years ago in England I attended an outdoor show of birds of
prey. There I saw a windhover, which is a kestrel, or small variety of
hawk, so called from its habit of hovering in the air. It was both exhil-
arating and frightening to see the kestrel and other birds of prey, like
falcons, climb high in the sky, hover and then drop almost with the
speed of a bullet on the faux prey supplied by the bird handlers.

I thought of Hopkins and his poem and of the image of a kestrel
that, for the purposes of the poem, Hopkins transforms into a Falcon,
with a capital *F*, thereby indicating more than a bird; it is, in fact, an

image of Christ the Lord, to whom the poem is dedicated. Using the language of medieval chivalry, Hopkins embarks on a poem that tries to express the inexpressible, the vision of Christ in the ecstasy of his passion. With this poem in particular, the question of who is a mystic comes into focus. Simply that Hopkins was a great poet does not make him a mystic, nor that he wrote religious poems.

But there is in Hopkins a point in certain poems where the transcendent breaks through and an experience akin to the mystical vision is evoked. Did Hopkins have a mystical experience in which he saw the divine light or glory of God that is normally hidden from our eyes? Or did his careful looking reveal the transcendent reality beneath all things? He once said, "If you look hard at anything, it will look hard at you." Is that mysticism or is the insight garnered from such keen seeing really the result of keen looking? In either case, what is seen comes from the divine element within things, so even if he did not have mystical visions, Hopkins would be a mystic in the broad sense, one of those who sees what we can only trust and believe is there.

Hopkins also saw in words themselves the mystery that words incarnate and reveal in certain combinations of our own making. As a poet he was a maker (which is the Greek root of the word *poet*). Therefore, he both received in contemplation and rendered in making what he had received. In the process a new vision emerged. For example, in this poem, as he is contemplating the kestrel, the poet receives an insight into ecstasy and suffering and how they are intertwined in the bird's gestures. In writing the poem, the further insight into the bird as Christ and ultimately as the mystic follower of Christ, as well, breaks from the page.

The very fact that the windhover reveals a glimpse of the mystery of Christ, bird and God-man merging in the poet's vision, says that Hopkins had mystical proclivities and was focused on Christ prior to seeing the bird. Christ was his all from the time of his entry into the Society of Jesus and probably before that, from the time of his conversion experience that led to his entrance into the Roman Catholic church.

We know from his own writings that Hopkins was profoundly influenced by the medieval Franciscan philosopher, Blessed John Duns Scotus, and his concepts of haecceity and intuitive cognition. Haecceity is the unique thisness of a thing and relates to Hopkins's concept of inscape. Intuitive cognition is how we grasp the thisness of a thing and relates to Hopkins's concept of instress. But Hopkins is most taken by Scotus' doctrine of the primacy of Christ. Following Scotus, Hopkins rejects the view of Thomas Aquinas that the Incarnation happened because of the sin of Adam. He believed the Incarnation of God could not be dependent on something so negative as sin. Christ would have come to be one of us and take possession of his kingdom, whether or not there had been original sin. As Scotus says,

> I say then that the Fall was not the reason for Christ's Predestination. Even if no angel had fallen, nor any human, Christ would still have been predestined—yes, even if no others were to have been created save only Christ.[9]

Because of the substantial union of human nature and the divine Word, Christ is first in God's intentions. He is the expression of the Trinity itself and of God's creative plan. Christ is the first conception in the mind of God, not an afterthought because of human sin that needed Christ to redeem human nature. The preeminence of Christ is exquisitely expressed by Saint Paul in his Letter to the Colossians.

He is the image of the invisible God, the firstborn of all creation; for in him all things were created, things visible and invisible...all things have been created through him and for him. He himself is before all things, and in him all things hold together. (Colossians 1:15–17)

For Hopkins this Christ is first and foremost the adorer of God. In one of his first sermons Hopkins says,

Reigning in heaven he could not worship the Father, but when he became man and entered upon his new nature the first thing he did in it was to adore God in it. As entering a church we bless ourselves, as waking in the morning we are told to lift our hearts to God, so Christ no sooner found himself in human nature than he blessed and hallowed it by saluting his heavenly Father, raising his new heart to him, and offering all his new being to his honour.[10]

In his first great poem, "The Wreck of the Deutschland," Hopkins introduces what will be the central motif of his work.

I kiss my hand
To the stars, lovely-asunder
Starlight, wafting him out of it; and
Glow, glory in thunder;
Kiss my hand to the dappled-with-damson west;

> Since, tho' he is under the world's splendour and wonder,
>
> His mystery must be instressed, stressed;
>
> For I greet him the days I meet him, and bless when I
>
> understand.[11]

This Christ whose mystery Hopkins says must be "instressed, stressed," is in all of creation, so that he can write in his poem, "As kingfishers catch fire,"

> ...for Christ plays in ten thousand places,
>
> Lovely in limbs, and lovely in eyes not his
>
> To the Father through the features of men's faces.[12]

Hopkins comments,

> It is as if a man said: That is Christ playing at me and me playing at Christ, only that it is no play but truth; That is Christ being me and me being Christ.[13]

It is this same Christ whom Hopkins sees in the windhover, which in turn becomes an "inscape" of Christ and an "inscape" of the poet longing to become Christ.

The best way to unpack what I'm saying here is to read "The Windhover" closely and prayerfully in the manner of *lectio divina*. The language of the poem is so dense, so original, and the images and allusions so complex, that we can only move through the poem slowly. First, the poem in its entirety:

> *To Christ our Lord*
>
> I CÁUGHT this mórning mórning's mínion, king-
>
> dom of dáylight's dáuphin, dapple-dáwn-drawn

Fálcon, in his ríding

Of the rólling level úndernéath him steady áir,

and stríding

Hígh there, how he rúng upon the réin of a wím-

pling wíng

In his écstasy! then óff, óff fórth on swíng,

As a skáte's heel sweeps smóoth on a bów-bend:

the húrl and glíding

Rebúffed the bíg wínd. My héart in híding

Stírred for a bírd,—the achíeve of, the mástery of

the thíng!

Brute béauty and válour and áct, oh, air, príde,

plume, hére

Búckle! AND the fíre that bréaks from thée then,

a bíllion

Tímes told lóvelier, more dángerous, O my chevalíer!

No wónder of it: shéer plód makes plóugh down

síllion

Shíne, and blúe-bleak émbers, áh my déar,

Fall, gáll themsélves, and gásh góld-vermíllion.[14]

As with holiness, we proceed now step by step. Hopkins capitalizes the word CAUGHT, a way of indicating that the word means more than just caught sight of. He grasped rather, in an instant, the inscape of the kestrel in the sky, its haecceity, or the unique gesture its life makes. He has instressed the inscape of the bird whom he calls morning's minion, or darling. The bird is also the dauphin, or crown prince of the kingdom of daylight, a Falcon that is drawn by the dappled dawn.

Suddenly the bird is no longer a kestrel, but a Falcon, with capital *F*. The Falcon is described in language reminiscent of medieval French chivalry and royalty.

The windhover rides the air with the ease and control of a knight riding his charger. The air is both rolling and steady. As is his habit, Hopkins is looking carefully; he contemplates. As the bird circles in the air and pivots on its wing, it looks like a horse reined by a trainer. And as the bird works the wind, with and against its force, it is in ecstasy. Then the bird moves off, and Hopkins uses the image of a skater's heel curving and carving a figure eight. It sweeps but hurls, too, two opposing forces.

The heart in hiding, meanwhile, stirs to be what the bird does: "Brute beauty and valor and act." The heart wants the inscape of the bird's flight—air, pride and plume—to buckle, which can mean to buckle together, buckle under or to crumple under stress and pressure.

It seems that the poet is saying to his heart in hiding that this inscape of bird and air, bird versus air, is what the heart needs to do in order for Christ to break forth in ecstasy in the poet as Christ does in this inscape, "a billion / Times told lovelier, more dangerous, O my chevalier."

When the bird buckles under the stress of the wind, its beauty shines forth with a radiance like the plow that shines brighter when it submits to being drawn through the hard, resisting soil, or when burned embers fall from the grate and break open, gash, in gold-vermilion colors. All of which are images of Christ's buckling under, surrendering to the Father's will, and then shining forth in the very act of dying on the cross when his body buckles under its weight. The very moment of Christ's buckling is his rising, as well, and will be the poet's rising if he can be in his own life what the Christ-Falcon does.

I believe that in his suffering Hopkins became what the Falcon does, not only in his inner suffering, but in his final illness, which led to the ecstatic resonance of his last words, "I am so happy, so happy." He had merged with the Falcon who is Christ. And I believe that his poems mirror the buckling under and the ecstasy of "Brute beauty and valour and act, o air, pride, plume." And in that Gerard Manley Hopkins is both poet and mystic whose holiness breaks from him "a billion / Times told lovelier."

reflection

Turn then, brethren, and give God glory. You do say grace at meals and thank and praise God for your daily bread, so far so good, but thank and praise him now for everything.... It is not only prayer that gives God glory but work. Smiting an anvil, sawing a beam, whitewashing a wall, driving horses, sweeping, scouring, everything gives God some glory if being in his grace you do it as your duty. To go to communion worthily gives God great glory, but to take food in thankfulness and temperance gives him glory, too. To lift up the hands in prayer gives God glory, but a man with a dung fork in his hand, a woman with a sloppail, give him glory too. He is so great that all things give him glory if you mean they should. So then, my brethren, live.[15]

chapter nine

Simone Weil, The Marvelous Dimension and
Baptism of Desire (1909–1943)

Just as the theology and life of the church derive from the revelation of God, so the theology and life of the mystic derive from a revelation of God to him or her personally. In both cases God takes the initiative in a given time and place to reveal the Divine Presence. When God is revealed to Moses in the burning bush, Moses himself, unaware and unsuspecting of the momentous occurrence that is about to take place, has simply been tending his father-in-law's sheep.

"Thus you shall say to the Israelites, 'I AM sent me to you'" (Exodus 3:14). God is pure existence; every other existence is dependent on that essential existence. And God is the one who sends. God gives Moses a mission: He is to be God's voice to the Israelites and to Pharaoh.

God's revelation to Moses was that of a voice, and Moses' life is to be a voice for God, though Moses himself is slow of speech and tongue,

147

a poor speaker; therefore, everyone will know that it is God's voice and not Moses' that is speaking so powerfully. He is to be a prophet, a word whose origin is one who speaks for another. And the God who reveals himself in Moses is a God who speaks from the fire on Mount Horeb. These are the gestures that will further define God and where God comes from: God is in the fire; God speaks from on high.

Each mystic will experience a similar personal revelation of God that will result in some mission: in the personal life of the mystic and in the communal life of the church. God takes the initiative; God chooses according to God's mysterious will. Mysterious because more often than not the one God chooses is not one we would ordinarily think of as worthy of a divine revelation. As Saint Paul says, "But God chose what is foolish in the world to shame the wise; God chose what is weak in the world to shame the strong; God chose what is low and despised in the world, things that are not, to reduce to nothing things that are, so that no one may boast in the presence of God" (1 Corinthians 1:27–30).

The mystic, in other words, like any human being, has not made herself or himself somehow worthy of God. No one is worthy of God's visitation. All the mystic can do is respond to so great a grace and say with the Virgin Mary, "[L]et it be with me according to your word" (Luke 1:38).

It is in this context, then, that I include Simone Weil in this collection of Catholic mystical writers. She never fully embraced through baptism the Catholicism she seemingly embraced in her life and social values. She was eccentric, emotionally damaged and probably even died of self-inflicted starvation. She was brilliant, but socially rude and difficult, overly critical of others and brash in her manner. But her life was an effort to respond to the needs of the poor and oppressed workers. And God revealed himself so tangibly to her that she was moved to kneel, for the first time in her life, in the Porziuncola, the small chapel of Our Lady of the Angels on the plain below Assisi, which Saint Francis had restored and later designated as the hearth of the Franciscan movement.

Weil was Jewish by birth, and Christian by inclination; she longed to be a Catholic, but, like so many, she never quite took that ultimate step. Her own tortured mind got in the way, her physical and emotional troubles, the inevitable passage of time while she vacillated. Weil was opinionated and aggressive yet compassionate to the point of choosing to suffer in solidarity with the oppressed. She was, in short, the sign of contradiction that many mystics have been. She was each of us who put off until tomorrow and tomorrow and tomorrow until there is no more time, and we die not doing what we wanted and intended to do.

As creatures we long for our Creator, the home of our making. But the very distance between Creator and creature is infinite, and only the Creator can close that infinite chasm. The pain of that divide, which is the longing, the cry for one's deepest roots, becomes itself the point where God meets us, not by presence, but by absence. We long for, and we are not satisfied, and that hunger and thirst becomes the proof of the existence of the one we long for.

Through Jesus the longed-for Other becomes one of us trans-formed by the presence of the Creator, whom Jesus calls Father. The transfigured Jesus is the image of who we will become by means of the passage, which is the journey of a life of absence from the Creator, provided we embrace that absence because it is the will of the Father-Creator whom Jesus his son reveals to us.

The mystic is the one to whom the Father-God has granted intermittent or even a single revelation of the mystic's origin and end in the midst of the journey of absence. The revelation is a presence in the desert of the soul so convincing that it cannot be a mirage, so real that it keeps the mystic soul in a painful longing for that presence always. And so the soul focuses on eternity, and in the process of that absorption in God, the passage itself is transformed. Even, and especially, in the absence of God on the way the soul is undeterred because it has glimpsed in this life the eternal life with God that is to come.

When the mystic experiences this eternal presence in the midst of absence (which is longing itself), and tries to express that experience, the inadequacy of words becomes evident. Only the language of metaphor can even hint at that opening of the veil of the ordinary word to reveal the God within and outside our ordinary experience.

The mystic stumbles and stammers, and these inadequate words are what we call mystical writings. And this poverty of words is so because the Creator has expressed from all eternity the definitive Word, who is the second person of the blessed Trinity, and who is tangibly expressed for us in Jesus Christ, who himself utters words that derive from his essence as God. He is the Word of God; he utters divine words preserved in the inadequate vessels that are human words, words unable to adequately express the one Word of God become human.

But inadequate words are all we have unless God chooses to reveal more to us. And this more is what we call mystical experiences: more than the words of God in Scripture, more than the words of God that are God's creatures, more than the images our own minds have conjured up. That more is what we look for in reading the mystics, one more proof of God's intimacy with us, one more way of expressing it, one more affirmation of the truth of sacred Scripture, one more absence in our lives if we have not experienced what the mystic has experienced, one more intensification of the longing for more. All of which has been succinctly expressed by the modern mystic, Simone Weil, in this wrenching, inadequate passage:

> Affliction is a marvel of divine technique. It is a simple and ingenious device which introduces into the soul of a finite creature the immensity of force, blind, brutal, and cold. The infinite distance separating God from the creature is entirely concentrated into one point to pierce the soul in its center....
>
> In this marvelous dimension, the soul, without leaving the place and the instant where the body to which it is united is situated, can cross the totality of space and time and come into the very presence of God.[1]

Yes, affliction, *the* mystery. Suffering as the point of contact with God. Not suffering sought after, but suffering embraced in love. Weil's life and longing are a powerful image of the paradoxes involved in this great mystery.

Mystery is the root of the word *mystic*. The mystic is one who is involved, who has journeyed into mystery. Affliction is what that "marvelous dimension" often looks like, its sometimes ugly, crazy face, its divine interior.

Simone Weil's is the story of a great mind trapped in a broken body and psyche whose very brokenness becomes her affliction, the point of her experience of the presence of God.

She is born in Paris to upper-middle-class, non-practicing Jewish parents, Bernard Weil, a medical doctor, and his wife, Selma Reinherz, an overly solicitous mother who has a phobic dread of microbes and who imposes compulsive handwashing on her children. She also insists that no one outside the immediate family is to kiss the children, one reason, perhaps, why Simone avoids most forms of physical contact all her life long.

Simone's only sibling is her older brother, Andre, born in 1906, who displays an early brilliance in mathematics, solving post-doctoral mathematical problems at the age of twelve. He later becomes a noted mathematician at Princeton University. Simone and Andre are close, though Simone believes she's intellectually inferior to her brother and often wishes she had been born a boy.

When World War I begins in 1914, Doctor Weil is called up, and Madame Weil, with her children, follows her husband to each of his postings. During this time Simone is educated by correspondence courses and begins to show signs of anorexic tendencies, refusing at age five to eat sugar because it is not available to the French troops on the front.

In 1921, when she is twelve years old, she begins to experience migraine headaches, which she will suffer without relief for the rest of her life. But in spite of her precarious health, Simone studies diligently and in 1925 takes her baccalaureate in philosophy from Lycée Victor Duruy, after which she enters the Lycée Henry IV, where she studies under the philosopher Émile-Auguste Chartier, who is better known under his pen name Alain. It is he who nicknames her "Martian" because of her evident devaluing of her femininity and the terrible intensity she displays in her intellectual pursuits.

In 1928 Simone enters the École Normale Supérieure, placing first in the entrance exams, followed by Simone de Beauvoir, a preeminient French existentialist author and philosopher. Here she becomes acquainted with leftist politics and demonstrates an extreme empathy for workers and their conditions. When she graduates in 1931, having completed a thesis, "Science and Perception in Descartes," and having performed brilliantly on her exit exams, Simone goes to work teaching philosophy at a girls' school near Lyons. For the first part of the 1930s, her writings focus on social problems and class issues.

She involves herself in public demonstrations on behalf of the unemployed, and in 1932 she is transferred to another position in Auxerre. Again there are problems, and ultimately her position is eliminated.

While she is on forced leave from teaching, she begins to work in three factories and soon learns how flexible human beings are. They easily change from feelings of anger or revolt against inhumane conditions to total submission. In contrast to the other workers, Simone feels that factory work is slave work in which the workers experience, among other things, the weight of meaningless time. All of which results in her own writings on labor that stress three elements for true dignity in labor: (1) the possibility of thought, (2) possibilities for invention, and (3) for the exercise of judgment.

The work and degradation of the factory so exhausts Simone that she agrees to accompany her parents on a vacation to Portugal, where she has her first real contact with Christianity. In a very poor fishing village she witnesses the fishermen's wives on the village saint's feast day processing around the ships, carrying candles and singing heartrending ancient hymns. "I have never heard anything so poignant," she writes, "unless it were the song of the boatmen on the Volga. There the conviction was suddenly borne in upon me that Christianity is pre-eminently the religion of slaves, that slaves cannot help belonging to it, and I among others."[2]

Simone means this very positively because of her deep compassion for those who have been made slaves by modern industry, especially the factory workers she labored with. "As I worked in the factory, indistinguishable to all eyes, including my own, from the anonymous mass, the affliction of others entered into my flesh and my soul. There I received forever the mark of a slave, like the branding of the red-hot iron the Romans put on the foreheads of their most despised slaves. Since then I have always regarded myself as a slave."[3]

Simone returns from Portugal, not to work again in the factory, but to teach at the lycée of Bourges, where she writes the bulk of the political writings that are published in her lifetime.

In the spring of 1936 she investigates the lives of rural farmworkers by laboring on a family farm in the town of Cher. In August she travels to Barcelona to join the Republican front. For awhile she is with the group under the head Catalan anarchist, Durutti. She also joins an anarchist trade union.

But Simone soon becomes disillusioned by the war and writes,

"[O]nce a certain class of people has been placed by temporal and spiritual authorities outside the ranks of those whose life has a value, then nothing comes more naturally to men than murder."[4]

By 1937 her health is in a steep decline, and her sick leave from teaching is extended. She travels to Italy, where in the spring in Assisi, she is moved for the first time to kneel and pray. "[S]omething stronger than I was compelled me for the first time in my life to go down on my knees."[5]

When she returns to France, she agrees to teach philosophy and Greek at the lycée of Saint Quentin in Picardy. There she continues to write prolifically, arguing more and more against offensive operation in war in favor of defensive guerilla warfare as more morally acceptable and effective.

In January of 1938 her health breaks down, and she goes to the Benedictine Abbey of Solesmes, where, while listening to Gregorian chant, the Passion of Christ enters her once and for all. There she meets a young Englishman whose face seems radiant when he returns from Holy Communion. He introduces her to the English metaphysical poets, John Donne, Richard Crashaw and especially George Herbert, whose poem "Love" she begins thereafter to recite to herself during her bouts with migraines. "I learned it by heart. Often, at the culminating point of a violent headache, I make myself say it over, concentrating all my attention upon it and clinging with all my soul to the tenderness it enshrines." She goes on to say, "I used to think I was merely reciting it as a beautiful poem, but without my knowing it the recitation had the virtue of a prayer. It was during one of those recitations that…Christ himself came down and took possession of me."[6]

These are the words that occasioned Simone Weil's profound transformation.

Love bade me welcome: yet my soul drew back,
    Guilty of dust and sin.
But quick-eyed Love, observing me grow slack
    From my first entrance in,
Drew nearer to me, sweetly questioning,
    If I lacked anything.

A guest, I answered, worthy to be here:
    Love said, You shall be he.
I the unkind, the ungrateful? Ah my dear,
    I cannot look on thee.
Love took my hand and smiling did reply,
    Who made the eyes but I?

Truth, Lord but I have marred them: let my shame
    Go where it doth deserve.
And know you not, says Love, who bore the blame?
    My dear, then I will serve.
You must sit down, says Love, and taste my meat:
    So I did sit and eat.[7]

After her experiences of Portugal, Assisi and Solesmes, God enters Weil's vocabulary, and she begins to give evidence of a particular interest in Catholicism.

On May 10, 1940, the Germans begin to move toward Paris, and Simone writes to the minister of education concerning what he means by "Jew" in the statutes restricting and reducing their rights. She is concerned mainly about how these restrictions might affect her personally. Simone seemingly does not speak out about anti-Semitism as such or speak up for the Jewish people who are being systematically persecuted and stripped of everything, including their lives.

The minister never answers, and on June 13 Paris is declared an open city, precipitating her parents to persuade Simone to go with them to the port city of Marseilles. Her brother goes instead to America.

In Marseilles Simone begins reading the Bhagavad Gita, a sacred Hindu text, which addresses her concerns about purity of action and motive in war, and she joins the resistance, writing for the war effort and helping those treated unjustly, especially Indonesians, who are being put into camps. She tries but fails to set up a frontline nursing squad.

Under the Vichy laws, Simone is dismissed from her teaching position, and her subsequent writings are dominated by contemplation of the supernatural and the mystical. During this period she also meets her spiritual directors—the Dominican Father J.-M Perrin, and the Catholic writer Gustave Thibon—in her continuing journey toward Catholicism. She teaches Thibon Greek, and she begins to pray the Our Father in Greek. When she recites it, she has a similar experience as with the Herbert poem. She begins to recite it every morning with absolute attention, and the effect of this practice is extraordinary. As she writes in a letter to Father Perrin, a letter she calls her "spiritual autobiography:"

At times the very words tear my thoughts from my body and transport it to a place outside space where there is neither perspective or point of view. The infinity of the ordinary expanses of perception is replaced by an infinity to the second and sometimes to the third degree. At the same time, filling every part of this infinity of infinity, there is silence, a silence which is not an absence of sound but which is the object of positive sensation, more positive than that of sound. Noises, if there are any, only reach me after crossing that silence.

Sometimes, also, during this recitation or at other moments, Christ is present with me in person, but his presence is infinitely more real, more moving, more clear than on that first occasion when he took possession of me.[8]

In 1942 Simone leaves her notebooks, which are to become *Gravity and Grace*, with Thibon and sails with her parents to the United States. For almost a year while she is in New York, Simone attends Mass every day. In November, 1943, she sails alone to England and eventually finds work with the Free French resistance movement in London. There she writes *The Need for Roots*, her last work, and becomes increasingly anorexic, which she attributes to solidarity with the occupied French.

When her health begins to deteriorate rapidly and she is diagnosed with tuberculosis, she refuses treatment and food. Though visited by a Catholic priest, she refuses to accept baptism. "I have always remained at this exact point, on the threshold of the church, without moving, quite still."[9] She had explained her difficulties with baptism in a letter to Perrin, dated January 19, 1942.

> I love God, Christ, and the Catholic faith as much as it is possible for so miserably inadequate a creature to love them. But I have not the slightest love for the Church in the strict sense of the word, apart from its relation to all these things that I do love. It is very possible that after having passed weeks, months, or years without thinking about it all, one day I shall suddenly feel an irresistible impulse to ask immediately for baptism and I shall run to ask for it. For the action of grace in our hearts is secret and silent.

> It may also be that my life will come to an end before I have ever felt this impulse. But…if one day it comes about that I love God enough to deserve the grace of baptism, I shall receive this grace on that very day, infallibly, in the form God wills, either by means of baptism in the strict sense of the word or in some other manner.[10]

No one knows whether or not Weil received baptism "in some other manner," for she was admitted to a sanatorium in Ashford, Kent, and died on August 24, 1943, of pulmonary tuberculosis and self-starvation.

Simone Weil, as extraordinary a mind as she had, as articulate are her writings on labor, on philosophical questions, on her own spiritual journey, is the kind of person whose contradictions and neuroses make one wary. She is intimate with Christ, who "appeared" to her, or as she put it: Christ himself came down and "took possession of me."

She is obsessive in her concern for the plight of workers, and she herself worked in the most demeaning positions in factories. She gives food to the hungry; she clothes the poor; she dresses and lives poorly. Yet simultaneously there is her self-disgust, her anorexia, her rough and rude manner that is critical and dismissive of her intellectual peers (though not of the poor and the workers). There are her incredible anti-Semitic writings that can't be explained away by saying she was a person of her own times. She went so far as to say that the Hebraic tradition was alien to her, that Jews were a people chosen for moral blindness, chosen to be the murderers of Christ.

Then there are the painful migraine headaches from the time she was a teenager, raising the question of the source of the visions: Were they self-induced, for example, by her extreme concentration and attention to Christ in the Eucharist as a way of blocking out the almost constant pain of her headaches?

Weil is the personification of the question often asked about mystics: What is psychological, autosuggestion, and what is from God? The only answer that satisfies in the end is Jesus' saying: "You will know them by their fruits" (Matthew 7:16). In Weil's case the fruits of her short, thirty-four-year life are staggering. Not just her intellectual output, her writings, as one would expect of an intellectual genius, but her unswerving commitment to and identification with the poor workers. Her compassion was so great as to seem pathological. She internalized their suffering, wanting to know personally their "affliction," a word she uses over and over in her writings. And in the final analysis, it is Christ who anoints her brokenness; it is Christ himself who takes possession of her, choosing, as Saint Paul says, "what is foolish in the world to shame the wise...what is weak in the world to shame the strong" (1 Corinthians 1:27).

But be that as it may, there is still danger in our emulation of mystics like Simone Weil, if we naïvely imitate their neuroses rather than the love, the charity that is their holiness. The affliction, for example, that was Simone's contact with God, is not ours, but hers. We have our own afflictions, our own brokenness, that becomes the point of our own surrender to or rebellion against God's will. We must take up our own cross, not Christ's, and follow him. It is the taking up in love that makes us saints, not the healthy or imperfect psyche that takes up the cross. It is the will to take up our cross, the will to surrender to God's sovereignty, not the perfection of the human being who takes up the cross.

Therefore, we look to the works of the mystics, the fruit of their love, not the eccentricities or peculiarities, even the prejudices, of their personalities. And in discerning holiness, one does not look for the perfect human being, but for the person's faith, hope and charity, despite all her or his imperfections. What is redemptive suffering in Thérèse of Lisieux or Francis of Assisi is sometimes viewed as neurosis in Simone Weil. Yet Christ took possession of all three of them, and all three had in common a passionate love of Christ and a heroic com passion for those who are excluded: the poor, the broken, the marginal, though in Weil's case she seems to have inexplicably excluded her own Jewish people.

Already when she was four years old, and Weil wanted no sugar because "the soldiers at the front were not able to get it,"[11] she proceeded to "adopt" a soldier and gathered bundles of wood that she sold to buy provisions for her soldier. Simone was so sensitive to injustice that still as a child she was upset by the way the 1919 Treaty of Versailles humiliated the defeated. A few years afterward she wrote to a friend, "I suffer more from the humiliations inflicted by my country than from those inflicted on her."[12] With that began her lifelong commitment to political justice and the end of what she called her naïve patriotism. Her passion for justice also explains her radical politics, her commitment to trade unions, why in the beginning she was enamored of the Bolsheviks and communism, and why she later rejected communism as being a greater enemy than capitalism. It does not explain her seemingly blind anti-Semitism.

Simone Weil was who she was. Like all of us she was a bundle of contradictions. It is not up to us to put restrictions on God's love and mercy. God will have mercy on whom God chooses, from the Pharisee Paul of Tarsus, to the sinner Augustine of Hippo. Weil was also her own person in that she did not meet Christ and the life she was living suddenly changed radically, as was the case with the rich young man Francis of Assisi. Her meeting with Christ only gave her consolation and intimacy in the midst of what she was already doing: her opting to live the life of the poor workers, her unstinting support and advocacy of just wages and the right to unionize, and her selfless attention to her students' welfare.

It was as if Christ himself was putting his seal on her eccentric, psychologically broken life. Even one so seriously ill of anorexia is embraced by Christ, affirmed for the good heart that persevered in charitable works, despite her eating disorder and debilitating headaches. As Saint Paul asks, "Has not God made foolish the wisdom of the world?" (1 Corinthians 1:20). God certainly did so in the brilliant Simone Weil, whose fierce intellect and unyielding persuasions were as nothing before the intimate presence of Christ.

One does not choose to imitate Simone Weil, but if one is broken and weak and continues to live on in love, Christ chooses you.

Simone Weil reminds us again that the mystical experience dispels the ego's illusion that it is in control because the mystical experience itself comes unexpectedly and has nothing to do with the mystic's making it happen. The mystic cannot force God's hand, as it were, or merit God's grace. God is pure gift, which, as so beautifully expressed by Jesus, is like the wind that comes and goes as it pleases and not as we command it to do. Ours is only to trust and believe that whether we are aware of it or not, God is there for us. "Consider the lilies," Jesus says, "how they grow: they neither toil nor spin; yet I tell you, even Solomon in all his glory was not clothed like one of these" (Luke 12:27).

The lilies cannot do anything to assure that God will take care of them, and this is what is so disconcerting to the mystic who has had an immediate experience of God. It reminds the mystic, and us who read the mystic's words or observe the gestures of his or her life, that we cannot control God, our lives, our world. Nor can one make the mystical experience reappear, re-happen. All the mystic or any of us can do is love God with our whole heart and mind and soul and our neighbor as ourselves; the rest is up to God. We cannot stave off death, we cannot make God appear in our lives; we can only surrender to the will of the God who creates, redeems and sanctifies us as God wills, not as we will.

This, of course, terrifies the ego, this letting go, this admission that we are ultimately helpless without faith in a being greater than ourselves, a being who holds us in the palm of a hand that is infinite, all-powerful, all good. The ego is convinced that just one more act of penance, once more heroic deed, one more technique will make us feel in control, powerful, confident, secure. Mystics like Simone Weil teach us that such is not the case.[13]

chapter ten

Robert Lax, A Sort of Bliss (1915–2000)

I mark my life with books. My first audiobook was my mother's voice reading *Huckleberry Finn* to her only child during the dark days of World War II, Dad away on the Island of Saipan, a mortar gunner in the Second Marine Division. A feminine voice, an absent father, a dazzling array of accents and voices in *Huckleberry Finn*.

When Mother read, I no longer felt alone as the New Mexico sandstorms wailed through the loose windows of our gray stucco house in Gallup. I wasn't there. I was inside my mother's voice, and we were both rushing down the fast-running Mississippi River on a raft, and America was opening up on the way. Mother and I were coconspirators running away like Huck and Jim into the wilderness of words.

And so it would go, book after book, until I took my first solo journey into Robert Louis Stevenson's *Kidnapped* and realized there was a voice beyond my mother's. It was inside the words themselves and I could find that voice all by myself. From then on I have always had a book nearby.

When I was thirteen, I began to read the lives of the saints, a world of saintly people braver and holier than I could ever be. The words about them and their own words I carried with me even as I stood behind the counter of Maria Ramirez's tiny grocery store on the ground floor of her house across the street from ours.

Maria would let me work behind the counter when she went up to fix supper, and I would read the life of a saint as I waited for the rare customer who might come through the door. One day, as I sat in the small darkened space of Maria's store reading G.K. Chesterton's *Francis of Assisi*, I knew my life was turning toward something more than the words I was reading, and that fall I entered St. Francis Seminary in Cincinnati, a place as far from Gallup, New Mexico, as the world of the saints, but as close, too, as their words.

Books being so important to me, I took books with me, and I found books there through all the thirteen years of preparation for the priesthood. They were not, after my first fervor, all saints' lives, or theological, or least of all, were they all pious. I'd learned, reading the lives of the saints as a boy, that no matter how holy the subject, it was cheapened or falsified or sentimentalized if the words were not authentic and good. And in college I learned that no subject was unworthy if the words were good and true.

I vividly remember reading Hemingway as an undergraduate and hearing my dad's voice, and the voice became more important than the story; when the voice faltered, I knew the story wasn't going well and the words were being forced. Again the voice gave me courage I didn't know I had. I would read *The Old Man and the Sea* to prepare myself to do something I was afraid of or didn't think I could do, like hitting a homerun one spring afternoon in college on rereading the story.

Words are that real to me, that important, as was again impressed upon me by the words used as America prepared to invade Iraq. While I realized that many good and holy Catholics and Christians approved of the war in Iraq, I did not. I was tortured by what the United States was doing, not only to the people of Iraq, but to words. *Propaganda and spin, propaganda and spin,* I kept saying to myself. *Hateful spin and propaganda,* as the TV droned on and bombs fell on Iraq and pseudo-justifications pounded over and over again the simplistic message that, yes, the end does justify the means; and no, a just war does not require that it be waged only as a last resort, when all nonviolent options have been exhausted; and yes, a preemptive, unilateral war against a vastly inferior military target is allowed. Any half-truth, any loss of life is justified, so long as freedom is imposed and then embraced by those whose gratitude and allegiance to the liberator is thereby insured.

As I continued to watch, everything I hold dear about truth and the word was being dismantled before my eyes, and I was beginning to implode from the sheer seismic shift in my perception of what is moral, of how language and morality are inseparable, of the healing power of words.

At the time I was teaching for a semester in the Franciscan Institute at St. Bonaventure University in western New York, and my growing despair and puzzlement, my determination to hold onto the Word, the source and validation of every true word, was temporarily assuaged by the discovery of the mystic and poet, Robert Lax. The St. Bonaventure University library holds the largest archives of Robert

Lax materials, a poet and hermit I was at the time only vaguely familiar with, mainly through his friendship and correspondence with Thomas Merton. I had no idea that in him I would find again the truth of words and the Word of Truth.

I began to explore the Lax archives in my free time and slowly began to feel my faith in words returning, my peace of mind being restored by words like these from Lax's *Peacemaker's Handbook:*

how	1:	lie
to		in
start		bed
the		for
day		a
right		while
		&
tips		
		look
from		
		at
the		
		the
mas		
		ceil
ters:		
		ing
	2:	
	3:	
	4:	
	5:	

—

be	bring
pre	peace
sent	
	to
to	
	the
the	
	mo
mo	ment
ments	
as	let
they	the
pre	mo
sent	ment
them	bring
selves	
	peace
to	
	to
you	
	you[1]

—

—

Here was language reduced to its essence: words reduced to syllables, words with double meanings when they are broken on the page: present becomes *pre sent*, and already there is a sense of mission in the very word "present." Here was someone I was immediately drawn to, someone worth reading. And so began my journey into the words and life of Robert Lax.

Merton and Lax had been linked in my mind from the time when, as a boy, I read Merton's *The Seven Storey Mountain* between customers in my dad's sporting goods store. Merton wrote of his classmate at Columbia University in the 1930s:

> Lax was much wiser than I, and had clearer vision, and was, in fact, corresponding much more truly to the grace of God than I.... [C]ertainly his was one of the voices through which the insistent Spirit of God was determined to teach me the way I had to travel.[2]

Lax's professor and mentor at Columbia, Mark van Doren, wrote of him,

> He...was so uncommunicative and so shy that even if I had tried I could have uncovered none of his secrets. His chief secret, I have since decided, was a sort of bliss he could do nothing about. Least of all could he express it. Merton has described his long, lugubrious, humorous face, and has said of it that it seemed then to be the countenance of one who contemplated "some incomprehensible woe." The woe, I now believe, was that Lax could not state his bliss: his love of the world and all things, all persons in it.[3]

As I began delving into Lax's life, it soon became evident that this love of the world and all things in it and his search for words to express that bliss defines the trajectory of his life. He was born in Olean, New York, November 30, 1915, and died on September 26, 2000, eighty-five years later, in Olean, two months after returning to the United States from the port town of Scala on the Greek Island of Patmos. He had lived as a hermit on the islands of Kalymnos and Patmos for nearly forty years.

Lax published his first poem when he was eleven and did some writing for his high school newspaper, but it was not until he entered Columbia University in the 1930s that he began to write seriously, encouraged and inspired especially by Mark Van Doren, and by fellow student Thomas Merton, who became his lifelong friend. Both Lax and Merton worked on Columbia's literary journal, *The Jester*, as did their friend, artist Ad Reinhardt.

When, a few years after graduation, Merton entered the Trappist Monastery of Gethsemane in Kentucky, Lax worked for almost a year at Friendship House in Harlem, a Catholic center for social work founded by Catherine de Hueck Doherty. He supported himself by contributing to and working on the editorial staff of *New Yorker* magazine.

On December 19, 1943, five years (to the day) after Merton had done the same, Lax was baptized in the Roman Catholic Church. Lax had told his mother of his intention the year before, and she only asked that he live his Jewish faith seriously for a year, which Lax did, even wearing the black hat and phylacteries.

At the end of the year, he told his mother that it was still his burn- ing desire to become a Catholic, and she gave him her full blessing.

The years from 1948 to 1951 were busy for Lax. He taught English at Connecticut College, lived in France and Italy, and continued free- lance writing. But the defining events of these years were his travels with the circus. In 1949 he traveled with the Cristiani Family Circus through western Canada, forming a special friendship with Mogador Cristiani, the acrobat and equestrian son who handled the family affairs; in 1951 Lax traveled with the Alfred Court Zoo Circus in Europe. The result of these experiences was his great early work, *Circus of the Sun*, and the later, *Mogador's Book* and *Voyage to Pescara*.

Circus of the Sun was written in the spring of 1950 in a basement room of St. Bonaventure University. One of the friars there advised him to write at the same time and at the same hour every day, which Lax did. He finished the first draft of the book at St. Bonaventure before leaving for France, but it was not until 1959 that the final version was published.

Of *Circus of the Sun*, Lax archivist Paul Spaeth writes,

> Lax, the reporter seeing things with childlike grace, at times relates his vision like an Old Testament prophet, at times like St. Francis composing a new "Canticle of the Sun," and at times like a kid wandering through the circus grounds eating popcorn.[4]

A deeply religious poem, *Circus of the Sun*

> is a reworking of the Genesis account of creation. The void is scribed by compasses and in this way given order. The compasses inscribe circles; later to be seen as the circles of the circus ring, the circles of the spheres the jugglers use, the circles of the acrobats somersaulting onto the backs of horses. The inscribed circle of the compass marks out a line where "beginning and end were in one"; the one being the creator God who, with wisdom, brings into existence all things.[5]

Lax's love of the circus began as a young boy when his father would take him to the circus whenever it came to Olean, and in one sense his whole life from 1949 on was a traveling with the circus, that Franciscan sense of wonder and itinerancy that took him to France and Italy and finally to Greece, returning to Olean shortly before his death, having come full circle, not only of his outer journeys, but of the journey of which he wrote in *Circus of the Sun*,

> Sometimes we go on a search
> and do not know what we are looking for,
> until we come again to our beginning.[6]

From the onset, reading Lax was like reading a Franciscan contemplative. His voice is that simple, that other-oriented. Franciscan contemplation submits to the truth of the other. It is a sort of obedience. As Francis says in *A Salutation of the Virtues*, Obedience is

> subject and submissive
> to everyone in the world,
> not only to people
> but to every beast and wild animal as well
> that they may do whatever they want with it
> insofar as it *has been given* to them
> *from above* by the Lord.[7]

This is the obedience of Lax. In a world where ideology often trumps truth, where the lens we see the world through is often more important than what we see, Lax is a wonderful truth-teller because he submits to the truth of the other, not to his own perception of or ideological lens to the other, but the truth of the other. He lets the other do

what it will to him instead of subduing the other to his own perception. Such contemplation implies the submission of looking and listening to the other until the other reveals itself. Once the uniqueness
of the other breaks through, we intuitively grasp its name.

Sometimes it is not a specific thing but an experience or constel-
lation of experiences that is the unique reality, as in this passage from
Lax's *21 Pages*.

> Something I remember about standing in the rain, on the street,
> upright, of course, and in the driving rain. Not driving, a vertical
> downpour. Night and under a light in the downpour of rain. Did
> I ask any questions then? Did I see a face? I was absolutely alone
> on the street. Alone. I was part of the rain. Not part of the rain,
> part of the moment the rain was about.[8]

Only someone wholly transported outside of himself into the other
could be so aware of "the moment the rain was about," rather than
what the rain was doing to him. The rain is not preventing the poet
from anything, delaying him, inconveniencing him, because he surrenders to it so thoroughly that he can't even remember what questions, if any, he asked. He's alone, but not alone, because he's part of
the rain under a light in the night. Light in the darkness, night that is
light, part of the moment the rain is about. It's *about* something; it has
meaning. He is connected to it. That is his bliss. And in reading these
lines, the bliss becomes the reader's. You are out of yourself into Lax's
voice and words.

A few paragraphs later, Lax writes of his vocation of waiting and
looking in words reminiscent of John of the Cross's "The Dark Night":

I open my eyes in the dark and see darkness. I close my eyes, even in the light, and see darkness. All the same darkness. Almost the same. Light comes and goes, but the darkness stays. Almost always the same. A fairly steady darkness. One you can count on. Almost.[9]

Almost. Because even darkness becomes a sort of light that is not darkness. "My observatory powers in the meantime had grown keener. I could see in the dark. I could see much further into the dark than before."[10]

Even of darkness Lax is positive, grateful, blissful.

My dark night of the soul, if that's what it is. My long night's waiting, if that's what it is. I saw a lot more then, on those nights of sleeping, not sleeping under bridges, sleeping, not sleeping on benches, under trees, in barn or on church steps than I'm seeing now. No matter. I continue to watch.[11]

For Lax the watching is all because,

I'm looking ahead. I'm looking toward some point, some vanishing point, or anyway, not yet visible point in the distance, in the future where something or someone I'd recognize would appear. (Where you would appear.)...

My person. My beloved, if you like; my sought-after-being, my remembered-one, would be there.[12]

I love that in this passage and throughout Lax's oeuvre, there is no mechanical, muscular working to attain some goal, to attain God, but a looking, a waiting, a receptivity to receive the other. Lax has no righteous sense of his own accomplishment in work or in prayer or of his own virtue. Instead all he is and brings is "A readiness to recognize you; that's all I've brought, that's what I bring to the encounter."[13]

And even then, even recognizing why it is he waits and looks in silence, he doesn't take credit for that stance. Rather, he says,

I didn't give up, because I couldn't. I didn't, because I was made to go on waiting. Made, put together, invented, born, for that single, singular purpose: to watch, to wait. There's no giving up on the thing you were made to do. There's no giving up on who you are.... I've wondered sometimes if you came, and I saw you, and I knew you were there, I'd continue to go on waiting.[14]

When I read *21 Pages* (and that is what they are precisely, twenty-one pages he wrote in the dark), I experienced what I've experienced in the authors who've had meaning for me and whom I read and reread: I trusted the author. I trusted his words, not just those of *21 Pages*, but eventually all his words, from *Circus of the Sun*, his first poem-as-book, to his final—I almost wrote Quartets, thinking of Beethoven and T.S. Eliot—minimalist poems that consist of two or three words, as in his beautiful elegy, "A Poem for Thomas Merton":

sin	sin		
gu	gu	one	one
lar	lar	cloud	hill
star	cloud		
		one	one
		star	cloud
sin	sin		
gu	gu		
lar	lar	one	one
cloud	star	hill	star [15]

sin	sin
gu	gu
lar	lar
hill	hill

Poet Ezra Pound's frustrated desire that everything would cohere in the end somehow does in Lax, at least it does for me. It coheres in words that return to naming, words that are more than words, words that identify the object the poet has become obedient to. In Lax words are the verbal incarnations objects become when they find their word, when they utter the word the poet hears, their singular, defining word, like "cloud," "hill," "star."

There is verbal transformation in Lax, from his *Circus of the Sun* to the minimalist poet he became already in his second book in 1962, *New Poems*, which for Lax the namer was precisely that, *new* poems. There the words, like Lax himself, are stripped down to their essence. What he does reminds me of something Octavio Paz wrote in *The Bow and the Lyre*.

Man's first attitude toward language was confidence: the sign and the object represented were the same.... To speak was to re-create the object alluded to.... Poetry presupposes a return to the original time.... [A] return to the identity between the object and the name.[16]

This confidence in the naming, re-creating power of words is at the heart of Lax's minimalist poems, as is the power of words to see. In a *Poets and Writers* interview in 1997, Lax said,

What I'm trying to do in my writing, is bear witness—not a false witness—to life as I see it, as I love it. Whatever it is, if it attracts me, and most of it does, if it's not hurting anyone or anything— I like to set it down.[17]

Bearing witness to what he sees and loves, like the mystics, and I believe Lax is one of them, he looks and loves and is therefore able to open up, uncover the mystery that is already there in things and people. The mystic uncovers and sees what most of us only see the cover of. And Lax the mystic spends his life looking, loving and recording what is there, and in so doing reveals what is there beneath ordinary seeing. He looks, he waits, and often something is revealed. It may not be a big revelation, but there's always some kind of revelation, as in this poem, whose title is itself a revelation of the poem to come.

On Seeing

(For Peter Walsh)

How to nail down

for the future generations

the absolute craziness

of a bird track in the snow

is, more or less,

if I may state it baldly

(and I must)

my problem.

Not that as a sign

this (same bird-track)

is in itself inscrutable;

but that a trace

of such importance

should be left

so casually here

on the road-side

(where he who runs may read)

is at least a step or two

closer to the problem.

What the fowl wrote

was

in itself

confusion:

heel-print of a creature

wondering where to turn.

Yet

in the snow

and sunlight

how resplendent!

how firm and delicate

at once!

how memorable

yet transitory

how worthy to be carried

(as it will)

from age to age,

this moment,

here recorded

of a winged thing

at a cross-roads.[18]

As I continued living with Lax's poems, I realized that for him making poems is a way of singing life. He seems wholly indifferent to publication or recognition. He wants only to make poems that give him the joy of a world made new by Love's words. Like a divine reporter he covers (or uncovers!) words, words which inner and outer events give him. As he writes in his Greek journal,

ah, he likes to write, likes to get writing done, likes to get things on paper...

sometimes he can hardly see why, but sometimes he does. getting experience—daily, day to day experience—on paper makes it more of an experience. breaks it into discrete particles and puts them back together again, lets him know here he is & what he is doing, and prepares him for whatever new thing comes along. gets him ready with his cups and categories to contain whatever new thing "falls from heaven."[19]

And what falls from heaven doesn't imply words superimposed from above on things. Rather what falls from heaven is the vision to see the hidden light that is in everything. There is that kind of sacramental seeing in Lax.

Now when things around me begin to lose their sheen or seem ugly or mean, I take up Lax, and light, like the inner light of an icon, begins to emerge from within things. This light is not a sentimental, Pollyanna-like fluorescence. Witness this entry from the Greek journal:

> i see a moth squashed on the wall. must have squashed it myself last night. first act on coming into the room. good business for character in horror movie. doesn't much horrify me when i do it. horrifies the moth. maybe horrifies the angels. thoughts like that then horrify me.[20]

That is the sort of contemplation that is at the heart of Lax. His unswerving, lifelong contemplation of things and events, naming them and seeing them from a perspective like that of the angels which consoles with the truth of his revelations, his epiphanies in the Joycean sense. The made thing, the poem in the broadest sense, becomes itself an object of contemplation.

> because yes—he likes to "write"—but to "do"—to do a particular thing—perhaps on paper (perhaps on canvas—perhaps in stone—perhaps, perhaps in a musical score)—a thing that will stand, a thing that will bear (that will sustain) repeated contemplation: a thing that will sustain long contemplation, and that will (in a "deep" enough way) reward the beholder.[21]

As there is the sacramental in Lax, which sustains me in ordinary time, so there is the journey, the quest, that is often eucharistic at the core, like the journey of the two disciples on the road to Emmaus in the Gospel of Luke.

Whether it is his journey with Mogador and the Cristiani Circus, his traveling to Pescara with another circus, or his journey to Marseilles and Greece, there is the culminating epiphany of a shared meal, a Eucharist. Lax celebrates every journey as if it were a further circus journey: the same characters, the same anticipations and delights in human performance, the folding up of the tents to leave, the overarching knowledge that this circus journey with its opening and closing tents is a microcosm of God's loving creation.

> Love made a sphere:
> all things were in it; the sphere then encompassed
> beginnings and endings, beginning and end. Love
> had a compass whose whirling dance traced out a
> sphere of love in the void....[22]

That is what I experience again and again reading Lax: a sphere of Love in the void of my own lack of vision. When I no longer have eyes to see, or care to, I reread passages like this:

> Have you seen my circus?
> Have you known such a thing?
>
> Did you get up early in the morning and see the wagons pull into
> town?
> Did you see them occupy the field?
> Were you there when it was set up?

. . .

Were you there when the animals came forth,

The great lumbering elephants to drag the poles

And unroll the canvas?[23]

When I read *Port City: The Marseille Diaries* (Lax uses the French spelling of Marseilles), I think of Saint Francis living in a new paradise with the lepers. Most of the characters of Lax's port world of Marseilles are those we would avoid, find less than attractive, perhaps even be repulsed by. But Lax is enchanted with these real-life circus characters, from Georges the Russian, to Theo to Fernand and Luigi, to Krevkor the dandy, to Raymond the panhandler, to the women of the port whom he draws with a Toulouse-Lautrec hand, to fat Dolly the artist with the mind of a sweet, hopeful child, to cross-eyed Giselle, who is sweet but not so hopeful, to Madame with her spitcurls and beaded earrings and high heels who sits and talks to the girls and the customers at night.

There is the picaresque, too, in Lax's journeys that reminds me of *Huckleberry Finn*, like this delightful scene from *Voyage to Pescara*.

The hill overlooked the neatly cultivated valleys, fresh and child-like in the morning haze. The monastery seemed to be deserted, but eventually I ran into two young monks, tonsured and wearing the brown robes of the Capuchins.

"Are you a tourist," they asked me.

"No, I'm with the circus. You see it below there?" The green tent in the valley looked big and was clearly the most living thing on the landscape.

"Is it a good circus?"

"Oh, yes!"

"Very big?"

"Quite big, yes."

"Many animals?"

"Yes, elephants, lions, tigers, monkeys, wolves, too."

"Imagine! Would it be a good circus for a monk to see?"

"Oh yes!"

"No vulgar acts?"

"Oh no!"

"No naked women?"

"I don't think so; it's a very nice show."

"Really?"

"Oh yes. You ask for me and we will get you some tickets."

"Are you sure?"

"Yes, we'd be glad to have you."

"Afternoon or night?"

"Whichever you like. You will see the animals. It's a very beautiful show."

"Maybe we will come down and just see the zoo."

"Good."

"Good then, we will see you later."

"Yes, I'll look for you."

I went down the hill feeling happy.[24]

What made Lax so happy, I wondered, in the face of so much tragedy happening in the world around him—race riots in America, the student revolts in Paris and Hungary, the disastrous Vietnam War? I look at my own life and see how upset and troubled I am by world events, by domestic policies, by political hypocrisy and decisions that consistently exclude the poor. How did Lax, who was certainly aware of the same realities, maintain such peace and joy?

From his poems and journals it is clear that his joy flowed from the decisions he had made. He chose to follow his own light always: He became a Catholic, he followed the circus (literally and figuratively) all his life long; he chose to live on Patmos as a hermit in the midst of the people; he chose to make poems, with no thought to their being published or not. The poems were but a daily choosing of a life-giving making that brought him joy because they brought him into the essence of things, that "dearest freshness deep down things" that Hopkins wrote of in "God's Grandeur." Yes, there is much that is wrong with the world; yes, people, and especially leaders, make decisions that make the world worse; but for all that, in Hopkins's words, there is that "dearest freshness."

> Because the Holy Ghost over the bent
> World broods with warm breast and with ah! bright wings.[25]

That is what gave Lax joy, and he knew it because he continued to make the decisions that enabled him to see with eyes that see and hear with ears that hear. These were decisions, not of escape from reality, but of going deeper into it, and their fruit was not a giddy happiness that is ephemeral, but joy that endures as long as one continues to choose goodness in the face of evil, life in the face of death, God and all God's works in the face of Satan and all of his.

In his looking and waiting, Lax, true mystic that he is, does not live apart from the poor, from the truth and simplicity of the first words of the first sermon of Jesus: "Blessed are the poor in spirit, for theirs is the kingdom of heaven" (Matthew 5:3). He welcomes always the stranger, the marginal, the poor one (materially or spiritually). Even on Patmos, though he waited and wrote nights and mornings, in the afternoons he waited for and on others who came to him.

Earlier in his life, he not only waited and welcomed, but like Saint Francis, he went and lived among the poorest of the poor. In Marseilles Lax lived for months, possibly for years (his chronology is blurred at times), among the poor of the old port city before leaving for Patmos, inspired by an icon of Saint John the Divine that hung over his bed in Marseilles. He wanted to begin a sort of house for the poor in Marseilles like Friendship House in Harlem, where he'd worked under the tutorship of Catherine de Hueck Doherty. Perhaps "worked" is not the word for someone who was by nature impractical and charm-ingly naïve, who spent his first few days in a Marseilles hotel before he realized it was a brothel. The joke among his friends at Friendship House was that he didn't know which end of the mop to use. "Lived among the poor" would more exactly describe what Lax did in Marseilles, or perhaps, "worked mercy with the poor," as Saint Francis describes his time with the lepers.

Perhaps Lax was simply a peaceful presence. Michael McGregor describes an icon among the images in Lax's hermitage on Patmos that defines what I see in the published poems (there are many still not published) of *Port City: The Marseille Diaries.*

> Above the images hangs an icon of sorts, a representation of the
> Russian Saint Seraphim, who holds a scroll on which is written,
> "Acquire the spirit of peace and a thousand souls will be saved

around you." Lax has adopted this saying as his motto—almost his mantra—slipping it into conversation at every appropriate juncture.[26]

And that's the way it was for Lax in Marseilles. His room became a gathering place for those who gravitated toward this peaceful man who had come to be with them.

luigi

runs for

the wine

georges borrows

glasses

one knife

one loaf of bread

one can of sardines

for five

and sometimes chocolate:

a single bar divided[27]

As in the Eucharist itself, what I see emphasized here is sharing, not just the meager ration of food; eating, not fasting; joy in eating simply and poorly, not the gloom of the ascetical curbing of wayward desires. This is why, all his life, the quiet, shy Lax attracted and gathered like spirits around him. He didn't evangelize or try to control or organize people. He simply lived his life of peace and others came to see and be near him.

Lax seemed to have lived out to the full what Merton wrote to him in a letter dated November 21, 1942.

> It is very good and sweet to be always occupied with God only, and sit simply in His presence and shut up, and be healed by the mere fact that God likes to be in your soul, because you like Him to be there. And in doing this you also love your neighbor as much as you could by any action of your own: because God cannot be in your soul without that fact having an effect on other people, and not necessarily people who have ever heard of you.[28]

Though he was a wise man and guru to many, Lax, in the words of Paul Spaeth, was a "wise guy, too. There's a lot of humor in his work."[29] Nowhere is this more evident than in his correspondence with Thomas Merton, a selection of which Merton published as *A Catch of Anti-Letters*. The letters are both serious and playful. Brother Patrick Hart, Merton's secretary, says of them that the letters exchanged their "thoughts on the world (including 'the monastic world'), the Catholic Church and society at large, and must be read as such. Throwing grammar, syntax, and spelling to the winds, they wrote lightly—yet wisely— as two supremely free men...."[30]

Here is an example of the kind of banter that went on between Lax and Merton, including the names they have for each other, which seem to change in every letter. Lax is writing to Merton, who's recently been in the hospital.

Kalymnos aug 11 65
Bien cher Feuerbach,
i am prized with sorrow when i see that while i was off at the

shootings in athens you were at that time fed by science in the hospital & forced to eat the ground-up innocuous foods, i am laffs again when i see that you are on a stumble across the hall from the co'colas & the milky ways, & that you are visited in your splatz by the tray-dropping jailbaits....

the gut tangle, as you've rightly supposed, comes from thinking too much & living in the wrong country. i used to get it everytime i'd set foot on the island of new york. this would often end up in the hospital, the clickety-clack down the hall & the wavery appearance of your friends in the recovery room.

it is good that they feed you only the mashes, you must be obedient to the mashes & the milky ways. always swallowing down the one & not neglecting the other. & you must act benignly, like a benign 50–year–old author, toward the small trembling girls & you will not be sorry, very small girls, like 8 & 10 stand outside the door & call my name all day, they do not invite me to their parties yet, but i know they will....

let me know if you are in or out of the hosp. let me know about the disc slip, too. is that all right? is it better? is it slipped back in place? 50 years is not very old for an author, you must stand on your head as much as possible & take care of yourself.

yrs,

Cardinal Mundelein[31]

So private in their language and references are some of their letters that they are almost unintelligible, being the secret language of a couple of imps having fun. They had nicknames for everyone and secret codes and always a different name for one another. One of Lax's names is Jack, as here in one of his light poems.

what
the
hell
is
this

jack

all foot
notes
&
no
po
em
?[32]

His small book *Moments* is full of humorous stuff like this:

42
you tell'em, goldfish,
you been around
the globe

44
in another life,
said the cat,
I'll be a human being,
I'll wash the dishes,
scrub the floors,
buy cat food,
do all the little things

62
you could tell from the way
he talked to Fido, he was trying
to engage the inner dog[33]

I mention this side of Lax both to demonstrate that he was not a pious prig or a wisdom figure in love with his wisdom, as well as to show why Lax was so attractive to others, to his friends and to the many who, like me, come to him seeking wisdom and find a lot of laughter and joy and discover that is his wisdom. Humor is the circus clown in Lax, the man who put on a clown's face in the real circus, loving every moment of it, like the playful Saint Francis preaching in his underwear or picking up two sticks and playing them like a violin. Like many of the prophets before him, Lax can laugh at the incongruities of life but especially at himself.

What of Lax's minimalist poems that consist at times of two or three words repeated in columns over and over again? There is a hint of what Lax is about in these two quotes from Octavio Paz:

> The history of man can be reduced to the history of relations between the words and the thought. Every period of crisis begins or coincides with a criticism of language. Suddenly there is a loss of faith in the efficacy of the word: "I held Beauty on my knees and she was bitter," says the poet. Beauty or the word? Both: without words beauty is ungraspable. Objects and words bleed from the same wound.[34]

And again,

> We do not know where evil begins, if in words or in things, but when words are corrupted and meanings become uncertain, the sense of our acts and works is also uncertain.[35]

Lax's minimalism, from *Circus of the Sun* to the simple naming of the objects that love's attraction draws, is a healing of the wound between words and acts, words and objects. He looks and sees and is obedient to the truth the other speaks. The other is more wonderful than my subjective projection onto the object, my perception of it. Only an ascetical and aesthetical selflessness can allow the other to reveal its unique essence, whether that other is God the creator or God's creature. He lets the other speak its word:

> one stone
> one stone
> one stone
>
> i lift
> one stone
> one stone
>
> i lift
> one stone
> and i am
> thinking
>
> i am
> thinking
> as i lift
> one stone
>
> one stone
> one stone
> one stone
>
> i lift
> one stone
> one stone
>
> i lift
> one stone
> and i am
> thinking
>
> i am
> thinking
> as i lift
> one stone
>
> i am
> thinking

as i lift
one stone
one stone

i am
thinking
as i lift
one stone

one stone
one stone
one stone

i lift
one stone
one stone

i lift
one stone
and i am
thinking

i am
thinking
as i lift
one stone:

one stone
one stone
one stone

one stone
one stone
one stone

one stone
one stone

one stone
one stone

one stone
one stone
one stone[36]

At first sight such a minimalist poem may seem simplistic and off-putting, but even as I typed this poem I felt its mantric power, which is even more evident when read aloud. And listening to Lax himself read his minimalist poems confirms his total trust in the word when it is the right word, the essential word. In Nicholas Humbert and Werner Penzel's video documentary *Why Should I Want a Bed When All I Want Is Sleep?* (Cine Nomad, Munich, 1999), Lax leads the camera into his hermitage alternating silence with simple words like, "one chair," "one table," "one bed," etc., that at first puzzled me. But then something began to happen. I started to notice each object Lax was naming in its silence and in the one word that is what it is.

After viewing the film, as I walked the film back from the friary to the Lax archives, I began saying to myself, "one tree," "one road," "one parking lot," etc., as if I were seeing them for the first time because I was saying their name, seeing them with the word that they were. What before had been but a jumble of things living or dead that one passed by in order to get somewhere else, suddenly became important in themselves.

It was like a return to Eden, where the poet had been naming things for me and then I took up what I'd heard him doing in the film. I thought of Lax's own words carved into his simple grave marker near the friars' plot on the hill above St. Bonaventure University. They seem to say very simply what Lax's life and work is all about. They show us how obedience, submission to the truth of the other, brought this modern Adam (and will bring us) back to paradise, where words and the lived life are one:

turn

jun

gle

to

gar

den

with

out

des

troy

ing

a

sin

gle

flow

er[37]

And there I rest: in those words, that voice, that injunction which seems almost impossible. Almost. Because it has been tried by saints like Francis of Assisi, who did in fact return to a paradoxical paradise of living with the lepers, of talking to the animals, of union with all of creation.

Perhaps like the words that made me feel less alone and braver as a boy, Lax's words are making a difference. Perhaps. Because though I've marked the last year with three more books, Robert Lax's *Circus*

Days and Nights, Love Had a Compass and *33 Poems*, and hear in them a new voice, a pure voice that is an antidote to the voices of spin and propaganda that do violence to the words and voices I have come to trust, I realize the hardest word of all is the first word of Lax's epitaph, "turn." Only doing the hearing will make a difference: turn, turn about, turn again. Return.

reflection

I am here for you. I have no other person
to be here for and no other reason to be
here. I am here at your disposal. Your
disposition. I have no desire except to
do what you'd have me do. I have heard
of other desires. I haven't heard of any
that mean as much to me as that. Haven't
heard of any that would mean as much to
me as knowing I was doing what you wanted
me to do. Or even not knowing I was doing
it. Simply doing it.

Why would I wish so much to do what you'd
want me to? Only because I think I was
made for that purpose. To listen & do.
To get my mind clear enough to listen
& then do what I hear I should do. How
do I know that the voice I'd hear would
be yours? How can I know that the thing
I should do is a good one?

I'd know because there's something I
know about you. I know that you love me.
I know that the things you tell me to do
are from love. You don't tell me to kill.
You don't tell me to die. You tell me to
love. You tell me to do the things love
does. You show me the way.[38]

Then Solomon said,

"The LORD has said that he would dwell in dark thickness"

—1 Kings 8:13

The Catholic church is not only the repository of a rich tradition of for-mulations about the nature of God, hammered out in councils and argued over by theologians throughout many centuries. It is a reposi-tory of a centuries-long spiritual practice, a disciplined way to God. Theology and practice are not something separate in Catholicism. They are complementary, as are dogmatic and mystical theology; they derive from one another. As the apostolic doctrine has it, there is no faith without works, no works without faith (see James 2:14, 17).

Within this framework and teaching are the mystics, those indi-viduals who have been graced with a particular intimacy with God, who has led them through a way that, though seemingly dark, is filled with the Light of the One whose light is so bright it blinds.

This truth is beautifully rendered in the following passage from *The Cloud of Unknowing*, a medieval work by an anonymous English priest writing to a twenty-four-year-old spiritual disciple who is searching to know God.

Lift up your heart to God with humble love: and mean God himself, and not what you can get out of him.... When you first begin,
you find only darkness, and as it were a cloud of unknowing. You
don't know what this means except that in your will you feel a
simple steadfast intention reaching out towards God. Do what
you will, this darkness and this cloud remain between you and
God, and stop you from both seeing him in the clear light of
rational understanding, and from experiencing his loving sweetness in your affection. Reconcile yourself to wait in darkness as
long as is necessary, but still go on longing after him whom you
love. For if you are to feel him or to see him in this life, it will
always be in this cloud, in this darkness.[1]

But one who perseveres in longing for God, even in this cloud of
unknowing, will eventually experience the touch of God, an unmis-
takable awareness of God's simultaneous closeness and transcen-
dence. One will know God's love and the message seems always the
same in all mystical literature. It is the message of Jesus: "You shall
love the Lord your God with all your heart, and with all your soul and
with all your mind; and You shall love your neighbor as yourself"
(Matthew 22:37, 39).

When God was revealed in Jesus, God was revealed in the cloud of
the humanity of him who was Jesus of Nazareth, who revealed himself
as the Son of God in his baptism, in the incident of the Transfiguration, in the bread and wine of the Last Supper, and after his Resurrection in his glorified body—all of these revelations given to those who
persevered in the darkness of the cloud of the everyday humanity of
Jesus, of the "stranger" who walked with the disciples on the road to

Emmaus, and revealed himself again in the breaking of the bread when he was invited to dwell with them.

Extraordinary mystical experience, though it is open to everyone, seems to be given to the few for the many. And like faith itself, the mystical life is pure gift of God. Nothing we do can merit either faith or this mystical "seeing" of God in the cloud of unknowing. Perhaps in the end seeing in the cloud of unknowing *is* faith. Perhaps the mystical life is recognizing the touches of God one knows only in the cloud of unknowing?

There are, however, those extraordinarily graced souls whose awareness of God is more than faith, those souls like Peter, James and John, who in the cloud of the mountain of the Transfiguration actually see Jesus transformed and hear the voice, "This is my Son, the Beloved; with him I am well pleased; listen to him!" (Matthew 17:5).

The author of *The Cloud of Unknowing* makes an interesting and compelling point when he writes,

> He [God] cannot be comprehended by our intellect or any man's—or any angel for that matter. For both we and they are created beings. But only to our intellect is he incomprehensible: not to our love.[2]

But aren't we created beings in our love, as well as our intellect? We are, of course, but we are also made in God's image and likeness, and "God," according to John, "is love" (1 John 4:16). If then we are creatures created in the image of love, by God's grace, we can return love for love and know God by loving God, rather than comprehending God by our intellect, "For who has known the mind of the Lord?" (Romans 11:34).

Furthermore, God himself became human to show us how to become like God in love. Love redeemed us, loved showed us the way in Jesus, who as a man dying on the cross, did not know the mind of the Father and cried out, "My God, my God, why have you forsaken me?" (Matthew 27:46). But then he "knew" the Father in love when he cried out, "Father, into your hands I commend my spirit" (Luke 23:46), and earlier, in the Garden of Gethsemane, "My Father, if it is possible, let this cup pass from me; yet not what I want, but what you want" (Matthew 26:39). As the Father surrenders the Son to humanity, so the Son surrenders his own humanity to the Father, and both are love. It is love that raises Jesus from the tomb and returns him to the right hand of the Father. And it is the same love that will raise us up to heavenly things and that will open us up to the touches of God's visitations, even in this life, if that is God's will for us.

Love, then, knows God in the surrender of the individual will to God's will. The Incarnation of God begins with that kind of love in the words of the Virgin Mary, "Here am I, the servant of the Lord; let it be with me according to your word" (Luke 1:38). An interesting variation. Not, "according to your will," but "according to your word," for it is the Word himself, the second person of the blessed Trinity, who is to dwell within Mary's womb. God's Word is God's will. She will give birth to the Word made flesh. And it is the Word who created all things and will, through Mary, create all things anew.

The Word is the expression of God's will. In Jesus that Word is written large so that we will know what kind of love it is that knows God and will be raised from the dead to live with and in God for all eternity. As *The Cloud of Unknowing* states simply, "If any man were so refashioned by the grace of God that he heeded every impulse of his [God's] will, he would never be without some sense of the eternal sweetness, even in this life, nor without its full realization in the bliss of heaven."[3]

What the author of *The Cloud of Unknowing* writes must, of course, be seen in the context of the teaching and tradition of the church. The church teaches that we can know with our intellect the existence of God, and philosophers and theologians like Thomas Aquinas and John Duns Scotus and others have brilliantly advanced proofs for the existence of God. But *The Cloud of Unknowing* is not talking about knowing *that* God exists; it is talking about a personal knowledge of God as God, and that kind of knowing is a cloud between me and God. Personal knowledge of God only love knows. Though God can and does reveal himself in a personal way that is extraordinary to certain souls, the individual never comprehends the divine lover, but can only respond in love, and know by love, so great a Love.

The mystics teach us that one who tries to know and love God sooner or later becomes aware that God is unknowable, but one can love God intimately despite God's ultimate unknowableness. With this awareness comes the further realization that all one's desire to know and love God has from the beginning been God's work and that, try as one may, two things are certain: You cannot find God who has already found you by running away from yourself, your own problems, your own unresolved fears; and secondly, everything you leave in order to respond to God's love is in the end redeemed, transformed and given back to you wholly new and in an unpossessive way.

It is as if you have returned to the garden of paradise illumined and purified so that you can walk again with God in the earthly paradise God intended for you from the beginning.

In this new life in God, God may seem most of the time remote, removed, but then just when you think the whole enterprise was an illusion, God touches you and you feel again the presence of the unknowable God who's been there all along.

The shape and dynamic of this journey to union with God has been talked about and written down for centuries. The particulars are unique to each person. God gives; we receive and respond. God removes God's tangible presence and we feel abandoned, unloved, terrified of the utter emptiness of life without God. God remains removed, remote for as long as it takes for us to know with certainty that the emptiness we feel when God is absent proves God is. And further, only God can make us know God has returned. We cannot merit or force God's hand, but God will return in subtle and unambiguous signs that confirm God has always been there, is now and will ever be our one true love.

The mystics represented in these pages have written down their own individual experience of this mystical, mysterious love, who is God, the creator, redeemer and sanctifier of every individual. Love is the way; love is the destination; for God is love. We know and experience God's love; we never really know God. We are led by God to love God for God alone and not for anything we can get out of God, including knowledge of God. We love and live intimately with God in a "cloud of unknowing."

Of course, something of God has been revealed: something of God in Scripture, all of God in Jesus Christ, but this knowledge is something we believe and accept in faith. It is not the knowledge of God as God. Only God can know God. What we can know are the loving touches of God in our lives and respond by loving God and everything God has made. That ultimately is what is meant by the mystical life.

Armstrong, Regis J., J.A. Wayne Hellmann, William J. Short, eds. *Francis of Assisi: Early Documents, Volume I: The Saint.* New York: New City, 1999.

Barclay, William. *The Gospel of Luke.* Philadelphia: Westminster, 1956.

Beever, John, trans. *The Autobiography of Saint Thérèse of Lisieux: The Story of a Soul.* New York: Image, 2001.

Biddle, Arthur W., ed. *When Prophecy Still Had a Voice: The Letters of Thomas Merton and Robert Lax.* Lexington, Ky.: University Press of Kentucky, 2001.

Bodo, Murray. *Through the Year with Francis of Assisi.* Cincinnati: Saint Anthony Messenger Press, 1993.

Claghorn, George S. ed. *Letters and Personal Writings.* New Haven, Conn.: Yale University Press, 1998.

Clarke, John O.C.D., trans. *Story of a Soul: The Autobiography of Saint Thérèse of Lisieux.* Washington, D.C.: ICS, 1972.

Daniels, Kate. *Four Testimonies: Poems.* Baton Rouge: Louisiana State University, 1998.

Devlin, Christopher S.J., ed. *The Sermons and Devotional Writings of Gerard Manley Hopkins.* London: Oxford University Press, 1959.

Flinders, Carol Lee. *Enduring Grace: Living Portraits of Seven Women Mystics.* New York: HarperSanFrancisco, 1993.

Gardner, W.H., ed. *Gerard Manley Hopkins: Poems and Prose.* New York: Penguin, 1963.

Georgiou Steve Theodore. *The Way of the Dreamcatcher: Spirit Lessons with Robert Lax: Poet, Peacemaker, Sage.* New London, Conn.: Twenty-Third, 2002.

Gorres, Ida Friederike. *The Hidden Face: A Study of Saint Thérèse of Lisieux.* Ft. Collins, Colo.: Ignatius, 2003.

Griffin, Emilie, ed. *John of the Cross: Selections from The Dark Night and Other Writings.* New York: HarperSanFrancisco, 2004.

Habig, Marion A., ed. *English Omnibus of Sources for the Life of Saint Francis.* Chicago: Franciscan Herald, 1973.

Hughes, Serge and Elisabeth, trans. *Jacopone da Todi: The Lauds.* New York: Paulist, 1982.

Lax, Robert. *Circus Days and Nights.* Paul Spaeth, ed. New York: Overlook, 2000.

———. *Love Had a Compass: Journals and Poetry*, James J. Uebbing, ed. New York: Grove, 1996.

———. *Moments*. Zurich: Pendo, 2000.

———. *Peacemaker's Handbook*, Judith Emery and Michael Daugherty, eds. Zurich: Pendo-Verlag, 2001.

———. *Psalm*. Zurich, Switzerland: Pendo, 1991.

———. *What Does a Stone Mean?* St. Bonaventure, N.Y.: St. Bonaventure University, 2001.

Merton, Thomas. *The Seven Storey Mountain*. New York: Harcourt, 1948.

Miles, Siân, ed. *Simone Weil: An Anthology*. New York: Weidenfeld and Nicolson, 1986.

Noffke, Suzanne, O.P., trans. and intro. *Catherine of Siena: The Dialogue*. New York: Paulist, 1980.

Paz, Octavio. *The Bow and the Lyre*. Austin: University of Texas Press, 1973.

Peck, George T. *The Fool of God: Jacopone da Todi*. Tuscaloosa, Ala.: University of Alabama Press, 1980.

Plessix Gray, Francine du. *Simone Weil*. New York: Penguin Putnam, 2001.

Undset, Sigrid. *Catherine of Siena*. New York: Sheed and Ward, 1954.

Van Doren, Mark. *The Autobiography of Mark van Doren*. New York: Harcourt, Brace, 1958.

Weil, Simone. *Waiting for God*. New York: G.P. Putnam's Sons, 1951. First Harper Colophon Edition, New York: Harper and Row Publishers, 1973.

Wolters Clifton, trans. *The Cloud of Unknowing*. Middlesex, England: Penguin, 1961.

Wolters, Clifton, ed. and trans. *Julian of Norwich: Revelations of Divine Love*. New York: Penguin, 1966.

Introduction

1. Regis J. Armstrong, J.A. Wayne Hellmann, William J. Short, eds., *Francis of Assisi: Early Documents, Volume I: The Saint* (New York: New City, 1999). p. 114.

Chapter One: Mary

1. William Barclay, *The Gospel of Luke* (Philadelphia: Westminster, 1956), pp. 9–10.
2. Reprinted with permission of the author.

Chapter Two: Francis of Assisi

1. Author's translation from *The Second Life of Saint Francis* by Thomas of Celano, VI, 10.
2. Author's translation of *The Testament* of Saint Francis in *Through the Year with Francis of Assisi* (Cincinnati: Saint Anthony Messenger Press, 1993), p. 82.
3. *Francis of Assisi, Early Documents, Vol. II, The Founder*, Regis J. Armstrong, O.F.M. CAP., et al., eds. (New York: New City, 2000), p. 542.
4. Author's translation of Saint Francis' "Letter to the Faithful," First Version.
5. Author's paraphrase of Saint Bonaventure's *Major Life of Saint Francis*, III, 3.
6. Author's paraphrase of Saint Bonaventure's *Major Life of Saint Francis*, III, 1.
7. Marion A. Habig, ed., *English Omnibus of Sources for the Life of Saint Francis* (Chicago: Franciscan Herald, 1973), pp. 730–731.
8. Author's translation.
9. Author's translation.
10. Author's translation.
11. Murray Bodo, *Through the Year with Francis of Assisi* (Cincinnati: Saint Anthony Messenger Press, 1993), p. 60.

Chapter Three: Julian of Norwich

1. Jonathan Edwards, "Personal Narrative," in George S. Claghorn, ed., *Letters and Personal Writings* (New Haven, Conn.: Yale University Press, 1998), p. 801.

2. Clifton Wolters, ed. and trans., *Julian of Norwich: Revelations of Divine Love* (New York: Penguin, 1966), p. 35.

3. Wolters, p. 90.

4. Wolters, p. 91.

5. Wolters, p. 92.

6. Wolters, p. 63.

7. Wolters, p. 67–68.

8. Wolters, pp. 71–72.

9. Wolters, pp. 75–76.

10. Wolters, p. 79.

11. Wolters, p. 79.

12. Wolters, p. 23.

13. Wolters, p. 70.

14. Taken from the card by the intercession slips in the Julian cell, St. Julian Church, Norwich.

15. Wolters, pp. 70–71.

16. Wolters, pp. 129–130.

Chapter Four: Jacopone da Todi

1. The poems selected and some of the mystical insights in this chapter derive from Alvaro Cacciotti, O.F.M., "The Cross: Where, According to Jacopone da Todi, God and Humanity are Defined," *Greyfriars Review*, vol. 9, no. 2, 1995, pp. 193–221.

2. Serge and Elisabeth Hughes, trans., *Jacopone da Todi: The Lauds* (New York: Paulist, 1982), Laud 85, pp. 243–244.

3. Hughes, Laud 68, p. 207.

4. Hughes, Laud 67, p. 207.

5. Hughes, Laud 40, p. 140.

6. Hughes, Laud 40, p. 141.

7. Hughes, Laud 65, p. 199.

8. Hughes, Laud 42, pp. 144–145.

9. Hughes, Laud 65, p. 196.

10. Hughes, Laud 65, pp. 200–201.

11. Hughes, Laud 42, p. 146.

12. George T. Peck, *The Fool of God: Jacopone da Todi* (Tuscaloosa, Ala.: University of Alabama Press, 1980), pp. 36–37.

13. Quoted in Peck, p. 69.

14. Hughes, Laud 82, pp. 239–240.

15. Hughes, Laud 82, pp. 239–240.

Chapter Five: Catherine of Siena

1. From Barbara Tuchman's *A Distant Mirror* (New York: Knopf, 1978).

2. Sigrid Undset, *Catherine of Siena* (New York: Sheed and Ward, 1954), p. 231.

3. Suzanne Noffke, O.P. trans. and intro., *Catherine of Siena: The Dialogue* (New York: Paulist, 1980), pp. 41–42.

Chapter Six: John of the Cross

1. Emilie Griffin, ed., *John of the Cross: Selections from The Dark Night and Other Writings* (New York: HarperSanFrancisco, 2004), p. 21.

2. Griffin, p. 22.

3. Griffin, p. 23.

4. Griffin, p. 23.

5. Griffin, p. 25.

6. Griffin, p. 25.

7. Griffin, p. 28.

8. Griffin, p. 29.

9. Griffin, pp. 3–4.

Chapter Seven: Thérèse of Lisieux

1. Letter 91, as quoted in Carol Lee Flinders, *Enduring Grace: Living Portraits of Seven Women Mystics* (New York: HarperSanFrancisco, 1993), p. 217.
2. Flinders, pp. 195–196, quoting Ida Gorres, *The Hidden Face: A Study of Saint Thérèse of Lisieux* (Ft. Collins, Colo.: Ignatius, 2003).
3. John Clarke, O.C.D., trans., *Story of a Soul: The Autobiography of Saint Thérèse of Lisieux* (Washington, D.C.: ICS, 1972), pp. 84–85.
4. Clarke, p. 98.
5. Clarke, p. 135.
6. Clarke, p. 148.
7. John Beever, trans., *The Autobiography of Saint Thérèse of Lisieux: The Story Of a Soul* (New York: Image, 2001), pp.135, 136, 138.
8. Beever, p. x.
9. Clarke, pp. 213, 214.
10. John Clarke, O.C.D., trans., "Saint Thérèse of Lisieux, 'Act of Offering,' " in *Story of a Soul*, p. 277.
11. Clarke, p. 271.

Chapter Eight: Gerard Manley Hopkins

1. W.H. Gardner, ed., *Gerard Manley Hopkins: Poems and Prose* (New York: Penguin, 1963), p. 27.
2. Gardner, p. 62.
3. Gardner, p. 12.
4. Found on a prayer card in St. Mary's, Oxford.
5. Gardner, p. 51.
6. Gardner, p. 60.
7. Gardner, p. 61.
8. Gardner, p. 60.
9. Parisiensa, III, vii, 4.
10. Christopher Devlin, S.J., ed., *The Sermons and Devotional Writings of Gerard Manley Hopkins* (London: Oxford University Press, 1959), p. 14.
11. Gardner, p. 14.

12. Gardner, p. 51.

13. Gardner, p. 154.

14. Gardner, p. 30.

15. Devlin, pp. 240–241.

Chapter Nine: Simone Weil

1. Simone Weil, *Waiting for God*, Emma Craufurd, trans. (New York: HarperCollins, 2001), p. 81.

2. Weil, p. 26.

3. Weil, p. 25.

4. Siân Miles, ed., *Simone Weil: An* Anthology (New York: Weidenfeld and Nicolson, 1986), p. 18.

5. Miles, p. 18.

6. Weil, p. 27.

7. John Tobin, ed., *George Herbert· The Complete English Poems* (New York: Penguin, 2004), p. 178.

8. Weil, p. 29.

9. Weil, p. 32.

10. Weil, p. 8.

11. Weil, p. xv.

12. Francine du Plessix Gray, *Simone Weil* (New York: Penguin, 2001), p. 9.

13. The outline for the narrative of Weil's life is from Kate Daniels, *Four Testimonies: Poems* (Baton Rouge, La.: Louisiana State University, 1998).

Chapter Ten: Robert Lax

1. Robert Lax, *Peacemaker's Handbook*, Judith Emery and Michael Daugherty, eds. (Zurich: Pendo, 2001), pp. 6, 8.

2. Thomas Merton. *The Seven Storey Mountain* (New York: Harcourt, 1948), p. 238.

3. Mark van Doren, *The Autobiography of Mark van Doren* (New York: Harcourt, Brace, 1958), p. 212.

4. Paul Spaeth, "Introduction" to Robert Lax, *Circus Days and Nights*, (New York: Overlook, 2000), p. 14.

5. Spaeth, p. 15.

6. Robert Lax, "Circus of the Sun," in *Circus Days and Nights*, Paul Spaeth, ed. p. 26.

7. *Francis of Assisi, Early Documents, Vol. I, The Saint*, Regis J. Armstrong, O.F.M. CAP., et al., eds. (New York: New City, 1999), p. 164.

8. Robert Lax, *21 Pages*, from *33 Poems*, Thomas Kellein, ed. (New York: New Directions, 1988), p. 188.

9. Lax, *21 Pages*, p. 191.

10. Lax, *21 Pages*, p. 194.

11. Lax, *21 Pages*, p. 194.

12. Lax, *21 Pages*, p. 197.

13. Lax, *21 Pages*, p. 197.

14. Lax, *21 Pages*, pp. 198–199.

15. Robert Lax, "A Poem for Thomas Merton" (New York: Journeyman, 1969), as quoted in Arthur W. Biddle, ed., *When Prophecy Still Had a Voice: The Letters of Thomas Merton and Robert Lax* (Lexington, Ky.: University Press of Kentucky, 2001), pp. 441–448.

16. Octavio Paz, *The Bow and the Lyre* (Austin: University of Texas Press, 1973), pp. 19, 25.

17. Michael McGregor, "Turning the Jungle into a Garden: A Visit with Robert Lax," *Poets and Writers*, March/April 1997, p. 81.

18. Robert Lax, *Commonweal*, July 12, 1996, p. 2.

19. Robert Lax, [from Journal C] *Love Had a Compass: Journals and Poetry*, James J. Uebbing, ed. (New York: Grove, 1996), pp. 224–225.

20. Lax, *Love Had a Compass*, p. 224.

21. Lax, *Love Had a Compass*, p. 225.

22. Lax, *Circus of the Sun*, p. 225.

23. Lax, *Circus of the Sun*, p. 29.

24. Lax, "Voyage to Pescara," *Circus Days and Nights*, pp. 162–163.

25. Gardner, p. 27.

26. *Poets and Writers*, March/April, 1997, p. 84.

27. Lax, "Port City," *Love Had a Compass*, p. 125.

28. Biddle, p. 89.

29. Michael W. Higgins and J.S. Porter, "Writing for Writing's Sake: An Interview with Paul Spaeth," *The Merton Seasonal*, Vol. 26, No. 1, Spring 2001, p. 19.

30. Biddle, p. x.

31. Biddle, pp. 309–310.

32. Robert Lax, *What Does a Stone Mean?* (St. Bonaventure, N.Y.: St. Bonaventure University, 2001), p. 33.

33. Robert Lax, *Moments* (Zurich: Pendo, 2000), pp. 44, 46, 64.

34. Paz, pp. 19–20.

35. Paz, p. 20.

36. Lax, *33 Poems*, pp. 56–57.

37. Robert Lax, *The Way of the Dreamcatcher: Spirit Lessons with Robert Lax: Poet, Peacemaker, Sage*, Steve Theodore Georgiou, ed. (New London, Conn.: Twenty-Third, 2002), p. 277.

38. Robert Lax, *Psalm* (Zurich, Switzerland: Pendo, 1991), pp. 8, 10.

Conclusion

1. Clifton Wolters, trans. *The Cloud of Unknowing* (Middlesex, England: Penguin, 1961), pp. 53–54.

2. Wolters, *The Cloud of Unknowing*, p. 55.

3. Wolters, *The Cloud of Unknowing*, p. 55.